Do it The Lazy Way

alpha books

1. Install a programmable thermostat. Adjust the temperatures once and you'll never do it again.

2. Keep small jars of clearly labeled touch-up paint for all your rooms in a shoe box, along with a small foam brush. Store under the kitchen sink for quick access.

3. Pour a pot of boiling water down the tub and kitchen sink drains once a week to keep them clear.

4. When it's time to install your window screens, wash them the same day you're washing your car.

5. Window washing services are inexpensive. Hire someone else to wash the outside of your windows at least once a year.

The Lazy Way
alpha books

*One luxurious
bubble bath*

The Lazy Way
alpha books

*Access to most comfortable
chair and favorite TV show*

The Lazy Way
alpha books

*One half-hour massage
(will need to recruit spouse, child, friend)*

The Lazy Way
alpha books

*Time to recline and listen to a favorite CD
(or at least one song)*

cut

Do it The Lazy Way

alpha books

6. Leaving for vacation? Shut off the water valves behind your washing machine. A broken hose can cause big damage and a lot of work!

7. Unless you think there's some nobility in mowing your lawn, hire the cheapest licensed lawn service to take care of it for you. Use your time some other way, and spare yourself the hassle of buying and maintaining a lawnmower.

8. To clear all the debris and leaves from your garage, use a leaf blower. Better still, have the guy you hired to mow the lawn use his leaf blower.

9. Squeegee your tile every time you take a shower and save grouting repair later.

10. Change the position of your furniture once a year to even out the wear on your carpets and floors.

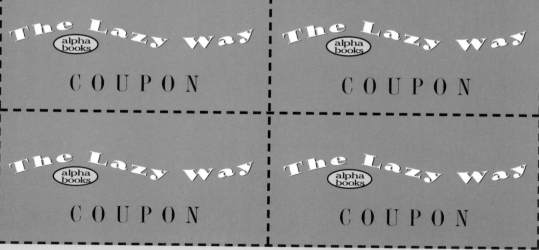

The Lazy Way
alpha books
COUPON

The Lazy Way
alpha books
COUPON

The Lazy Way
alpha books
COUPON

The Lazy Way
alpha books
COUPON

Care For Your Home

The Lazy Way ™

Care For Your Home

Terry Meany

Macmillan • USA

Macmillan Publishing books may be purchased for business or sales promotional use. For information please write: Special Markets Department, Macmillan Publishing USA, 1633 Broadway, New York, NY 10019.

International Standard Book Number: 0-02-862646-x
Library of Congress Catalog Card Number: 98-88079

00 99 98   8 7 6 5 4 3 2 1

Interpretation of the printing code: the rightmost number of the first series of numbers is the year of the book's printing; the rightmost number of the second series of numbers is the number of the book's printing. For example, a printing code of 98-1 shows that the first printing occurred in 1998.

Printed in the United States of America

Page creation by Carrie Allen, Eric Brinkman, and Heather Pope.

You Don't Have to Feel Guilty Anymore!

IT'S O.K. TO DO IT *THE LAZY WAY!*

It seems every time we turn around, we're given more responsibility, more information to absorb, more places we need to go, and more numbers, dates, and names to remember. Both our bodies and our minds are already on overload. And we know what happens next—cleaning the house, balancing the checkbook, and cooking dinner get put off until "tomorrow" and eventually fall by the wayside.

So let's be frank—we're all starting to feel a bit guilty about the dirty laundry, stacks of ATM slips, and Chinese take-out. Just thinking about tackling those terrible tasks makes you exhausted, right? If only there were an easy, effortless way to get this stuff done! (And done right!)

There is—*The Lazy Way*! By providing the pain-free way to do something—including tons of shortcuts and time-saving tips, as well as lists of all the stuff you'll ever need to get it done efficiently—*The Lazy Way* series cuts through all of the time-wasting thought processes and laborious exercises. You'll discover the secrets of those who have figured out *The Lazy Way*. You'll get things done in half the time it takes the average person—and then you will sit back and smugly consider those poor suckers who haven't discovered *The Lazy Way* yet. With *The Lazy Way*, you'll learn how to put in minimal effort and get maximum results so you can devote your attention and energy to the pleasures in life!

THE LAZY WAY PROMISE

Everyone on *The Lazy Way* staff promises that, if you adopt *The Lazy Way* philosophy, you'll never break a sweat, you'll barely lift a finger, you won't put strain on your brain, and you'll have plenty of time to put up your feet. We guarantee you will find that these activities are no longer hardships, since you're doing them *The Lazy Way*. We also firmly support taking breaks and encourage rewarding yourself (we even offer our suggestions in each book!). With *The Lazy Way*, the only thing you'll be overwhelmed by is all of your newfound free time!

THE LAZY WAY SPECIAL FEATURES

Every book in our series features the following sidebars in the margins, all designed to save you time and aggravation down the road.

- **"Quick n' Painless"**—shortcuts that get the job done fast.
- **"You'll Thank Yourself Later"**—advice that saves time down the road.
- **"A Complete Waste of Time"**—warnings that spare countless headaches and squandered hours.
- **"If You're So Inclined"**—optional tips for moments of inspired added effort.
- **"The Lazy Way"**—rewards to make the task more pleasurable.

If you've either decided to give up altogether or have taken a strong interest in the subject, you'll find information on hiring outside help with "How to Get Someone Else to Do It" as well as further reading recommendations in "If You Want to Learn More, Read These." In addition, there's an only-what-you-need-to-know glossary of terms and product names ("If You Don't Know What It Means/Does, Look Here") as well as "It's Time for Your Reward"—fun and relaxing ways to treat yourself for a job well done.

With *The Lazy Way* series, you'll find that getting the job done has never been so painless!

Series Editor
Amy Gordon

Editorial Director
Gary Krebs

Director of Creative Services
Michele Laseau

Cover Designer
Michael Freeland

Managing Editor
Robert Shuman

Production Editor
Robyn Burnett

Development Editor
Doris Cross

What's in This Book

Staying Out of the Doghouse

Every day in every way you may be getting better, but your house is not. Your dwelling is kind of like the scruffy little puppy you may have had as a kid; he depended on you to tend to him and keep him happy. If you didn't, he could make your life miserable. Think of your house as a puppy.

Your house is the biggest single investment you may ever make. Unlike stocks and bonds, whose activities, however erratic, get recorded quietly in monthly reports, houses moan and groan and demand constant attention. But your house isn't content to let you live in it and be comfortable. It wants to be painted and cleaned and get immediate first aid for its wounds—in the form of plaster and carpet and roofing shingles—until its next playful mishap. You have to live somewhere and a house has many advantages, so stop feeling guilty about failing to satisfy its demands. Learn to meet them the Lazy Way.

This guide assumes that you're intelligent and responsible. You like your house and want to take good care of it. But you don't have a lot of spare time, and you'd rather be (you fill this in)_____ than cleaning the gutters or repairing a broken lock. You know something about how to fix things, but you have a life, and a pretty full one. This book will show you easier and quicker ways to keep your house well-maintained without having to make a second career of it.

The first line of defense is preventive maintenance—getting to problems before they get to you. That means spending less time on repairs. Unfortunately, it doesn't mean that you'll never have to find a leak or fix a floorboard again. Things break, and Mother Nature has a lot to say about how long your shingles will last.

So when you have to fix something—anything, big or small—just find the chapter that shows you what tools you'll need and how to make the job hassle-free. And if you're really lazy (smart), you'll avail yourself of the wisdom you'll find in boxes on every pages. You can get advice about shortcuts, optional mini-projects, mistakes you might otherwise make, and how to make caring for your home less of a chore and more of a pleasure.

Congratulations! Now you'll have the extra time and energy to spend on the other important things in your life.

Part 1

Less Is More: A Few Good Tools

Are You Too Lazy to Read "A Few Good Tools?"

1 The only tools you understand come on a Swiss army knife.
☐ yes ☐ no

2 If someone says "screwdriver" you think vodka and orange juice.
☐ yes ☐ no

3 You think that hardware stores sell computer parts. ☐ yes ☐ no

Tools to Move the Job Along

"**U**se the right tool for the job" is a compelling mantra. It must be transmitted subliminally by covert means to shoppers at home improvement centers all over the country. Why else would weekend carpenters who want to build a planter box walk out with five-horsepower worm-drive circular saws and cordless drills powered by triple nuclear-activated cadmium battery packs?

Most of the tools you'll need for normal home maintenance will fit inside a single tool box. Tools that you're only going to use once or occasionally should be borrowed or rented. Who wants to clutter up the garage with a table saw you only needed for one job?

Tools can be divided into different types. There are manual tools and power tools, tools that cut, grind, drill, pull things apart and tools that put things together. The condition of your house will determine what tools you need. If you have old plumbing, you may need a few pipe wrenches. If your

3

YOU'LL THANK YOURSELF LATER

Fight the urge to buy fancy tools you don't really need! It's easier to think your project through first, figure out what tools you'll need, then decide which to rent or borrow. Otherwise, that belt sander you swore you needed might gather dust until your next garage sale.

house is new, a Swiss army knife may be the tool you use most. If that's a little *too* basic for you, here's a list of tools you should have whether your house is icons for old, middle-aged, or new.

There's more information ahead about what they're used for.

TOOLS—MUST HAVES

- Rubbermaid tool box
- Medium-weight claw hammer
- Needle-nose pliers
- Large channel-lock pliers
- Wire cutters
- Measuring tape
- Utility knife
- Flashlight
- Stud finder
- Lineman's pliers
- Screwdrivers: Multi-bit screwdriver with different sized slotted and Phillips bits
- Small jeweler's set
- Crescent wrench
- Nail set or punch
- Allen wrenches

If some of these names are unfamiliar, you'll probably recognize the tools when you see them. Shopping for them is simple!

1. Go to your local hardware or home improvement store.

2. Take a leisurely tour of the tool section.

3. Try out different sizes. Be sure whatever you buy is comfortable in your hands.

4. You don't need the most expensive tools for only occasional use.

One medium-sized tool box will hold all of these tools. Here's how they'll help speed up your house upkeep.

What Must-Have Tools Do

Rubbermaid tool box: A plastic tool box, such as Rubbermaid's, has some advantages over a metal tool box. It's lighter in weight, doesn't have any sharp edges, and tends to be more durable than an inexpensive metal box. You can even get some that double as step stools!

Hammer: Pounds nails in, pulls them out. A claw hammer will do both functions well. Try several to find one comfortable for your grip and one that isn't too heavy for you to swing easily.

Channel-lock pliers: These come in different sizes, so buy a large pair. They are useful for loosening up plumbing fixtures, especially traps under sinks, that sometimes have to be removed to clear obstructions. They can also be used to loosen tight jar lids.

QUICK 🔘 PAINLESS

If you're not too sure of yourself, show your list to a friendly clerk, but be sure that whatever you buy feels comfortable in your hands.

- Needle-nose pliers: Long, narrow grabbers, good for holding small parts or bending wires in electrical outlets or switches. Buy a medium-sized pair.

- Wire cutters: For cutting anything from stereo speaker wires to picture frame wire. A large size will be more versatile.

- Measuring tape: Get at least a 12-foot tape (but a 25-foot tape is better) with a self-locking feature. This prevents the extended tape from returning to the case until you release it.

- Utility knife: A razor knife. Used for stripping insulation from wires, cutting up cardboard, or cutting matting for pictures and paintings. Buy one with a retractable blade.

- Razor scraper: For scraping paint and putty off glass, getting sticky labels off things, etc. Buy one with a retractable blade.

- Flashlight: You can never find one when you need one, so consider getting two. Better yet, some now come in packages of three or four flashlights at good prices. Keep several around the house for the next blackout!

- Stud finder: Used to find wall studs prior to hanging pictures or shelves (you want to secure to a stud, not to the plaster or wallboard, if possible). The simplest ones have a magnet and a directional indicator. The better ones are battery operated and more reliable.

- Lineman's pliers: Good for gripping and cutting wire.

QUICK ʙ PAINLESS

If you loan your tools out, take a lesson from the contractors. Mark them with spray paint so the borrower will give them back. A bright day-glo color works well. Bright colored tape might be a little neater.

- Screwdrivers: Buy several inexpensive slotted and Phillips types. Easier still, buy the type that comes with interchangeable bits, both slotted and Phillips, and have two-in-one! Ideally, have many different sizes of slotted and Phillips bits.

- Jeweler's set: Useful for small repairs (eyeglasses, electronics, etc.) and costs only about two bucks.

- Crescent wrench: Its head adjusts to accommodate different sizes of nuts and bolts. Useful for some plumbing work and bicycle repair. Buy a medium-sized wrench.

- Nail set: A steel punch that you tap with a hammer to set finish nails so the heads no longer show above the surface. Buy a packaged set of three.

- Allen wrenches: Small, L-shaped hexagonal wrenches. You only need a small set to tighten the increasing amount of stuff in our lives (bicycle parts, self-assembled furniture) that use Allen bolts.

Good-Idea Tools

Well, this list could go on forever! It's always a good idea to have a tool around for the one time you need it, but you end up with drawers full of never-to-be-used-again linoleum knives, tack hammers, and tin snips. If you live in a neighborhood of older homes, there's always a neighbor who has one of every tool ever manufactured in the Western hemisphere. It's easier to borrow a jigsaw and take it back with a plate of cookies than it is to buy one and wonder when you're ever going to use it again!

QUICK 🔘 PAINLESS

If your home is new or newer, consider buying a pre-packaged tool kit, available at most home centers. Tools come in slim, briefcase-like plastic cases and often include a hammer, pliers, wrench, screwdriver, measuring tape, and fasteners. For around $25, these can't be beat!

Regular masking tape can be difficult to remove after 24 hours— even less if it's in direct sunlight. Keep this in mind if you tape it to painted surfaces.

A list of Good-Idea Tools would include:

- Spray lubricant (WD-40 or silicone)
- Masking tape and electrician's tape
- Small magnet
- Putty knife
- Small mirror
- Sandpaper (various grits) and steel-wool
- Handsaw
- Hacksaw blades
- Circuit tester
- 25-foot or 50-foot 12/2 extension cord

These tools take up a little more room than the essential list, but should fit cozily in a wooden wine crate. Why would you need a small mirror or magnet? To make your life easier! Read on.

Good-Idea Tool Uses

- Spray lubricant: Dozens (and dozens!) of uses. One quick spray and it's the end of that annoying squeaky door hinge. Sticky locks? A quick shot of spray silicone or WD-40 and it's smooth sailing. Use it on garage door tracks once a month or so, too!

- Masking tape/electrician's tape: Wrapping packages, labeling boxes, even use as a cheap fly catcher— masking tape does it all! You may not be wiring your house, but electrician's tape comes in handy for patching lamp cords (like the ones you might have caught in your vacuum cleaner).

- Small magnet: Use one of these to clean up spilled nails or screws. Also, when you're looking at antique hardware, a magnet will tell you if the metal is solid brass or brass-plated (a magnet won't stick to brass because brass is nonferrous).

- Putty knife: Use for all small wall repairs, epoxy work, window glazing, and minor paint scraping. Buy a knife with a flexible metal blade.

- Small mirror: Perfect for looking into inaccessible spaces or for adjusting a TV picture when the controls are on the back of the set.

- Sandpaper/steel wool: Use sandpaper for sanding away those pesky splinters on your deck or for sanding wall repair patches. Steel wool can rub away rust stains and clean stubborn stains in your oven.

- Handsaw: A small finishing saw will do for those unexpected woodworking projects.

- Hacksaw blades: When you need to do very fine cutting, these will do the trick.

- Circuit tester: An inexpensive, simple two-pronged probe that will light up if a circuit is "hot" (power is on). This will tell you if your problem is a lack of power or is with the item that is plugged in.

- Extension cord: Wire is measured by its thickness or gauge, and extension cords are marked accordingly. A 12/2 extension cord is twelve gauge, which will carry more than enough power to electric tools and small appliances. It is important that the extension

IF YOU'RE SO
INCLINED

Are you a garage-sale addict? Do your tool shopping at the same time! Estate sales almost always have odds and ends of common tools. This can be a fun way of gathering the tools you need, and less expensive too!

cord be able to meet the electrical demand of whatever is plugged into it, so buy a twelve-gauge cord at least 25 feet long.

Tools are a terrific bargain. A hammer can last for generations. When was the last time someone said that about a PC? Follow these lists and you'll have the tools to make your house maintenance smooth and easy.

YOU'LL THANK YOURSELF LATER

If you loan your tools, make the borrower sign the tool out. Otherwise, one of you will forget, and you'll end up replacing it. Trust me on this one.

Getting Time on Your Side

	The Old Way	The Lazy Way
Buying tools	30 minutes each trip	60 minutes, 1 trip
Sanding a door with sander	45 minutes by hand	10 minutes
Finding tools	10–15 minutes	2 minutes
Sawing a sheet of plywood	About 2 coffee breaks	Between slurps
Sawing straight through a piece of plywood	Never	Better than even odds
Finding Dad something he likes for Father's Day	Good luck	Oh, boy, a tool!

Chapter two

No-Sweat Power Tools

Rome wasn't built in a day, but it would have been built a lot faster if The Home Depot had been around. Romulus and Remus would have been down there every morning filling up great wooden carts with paving stones, slabs of marble, and lead plumbing fixtures. Banners announcing "LX Days' Financing Same as Cash" would draw palace owners all the way from Carthage. Power tools for cutting stone, mixing concrete, and drilling holes would have made labor costs negligible.

The plethora of power tools available today would make any medieval guild member toss his block planes aside and start clamoring for electricity. Power tools have relieved much of the drudgery of building and repair work while improving quality. A power miter saw, for example, will always cut straighter than a hand saw, so a less experienced woodworker can still get top results.

How does this affect you and your house? An electric drill will make a cleaner, neater hole for that stereo speaker wire you want to pass through a wall, and do it a lot faster than if

you tried to whittle your way through it with a "barbecue skewer." How about that weathered front door you need to touch up or refinish? An electric finishing sander makes quick work of old varnish and worn wood.

There are a lot of specialized power tools to choose from, but you'll only need to buy a few for your home projects. Later we'll talk about the ones you may need only once or twice and are better off renting or borrowing.

POWER TOOLS FOR NOBODY'S FOOLS

- 3/8" drill
- Orbital finishing sander
- Blower

Power Power

A 3/8" drill will cover most of your needs. Drills are manufactured by chuck size. The chuck holds the drill bit or drill attachment. The larger the chuck, the larger the drill motor since you need more power to drive larger drill bits. Stick with a 3/8" size rather than the smaller 1/4" drills. They can be, shall we say, performance-impaired when it comes to some drilling jobs.

In addition to drilling holes, drills can accommodate a number of attachments for sanding, cleaning, and polishing. Prices are all over the board, from around $30 to more than $150. A medium-priced electric drill in the $50–$60 dollar range will satisfy most requirements. For minor drilling, buy an even less expensive model. Cordless drills work off batteries and are wonderfully convenient, but the batteries need recharging, sometimes before you've finished your chore! Professionals always buy an extra battery so one is being charged while the other is in use. If you can justify buying a second battery, by all means do. It's better than waiting around for the charger light to go off.

- **Orbital sander:** Also called speedblocks, these finishing sanders are a marvel. They produce a finer, more refined finish than a drill's disc attachment. A piece of sandpaper is fitted over a rubber pad and moves in small, rapid orbits, reducing to a fraction the time and effort of hand sanding. These sanders will eat through old finishes and splinters effortlessly. All you do is guide them and let them do the work. Some people even use them for back massages—using a thick towel over the sanding pad—but you can be sure the manufacturer won't recommend them for that! Using a speedblock will leave small orbital marks. They won't be really noticeable if you're going to paint the surface, but on wood you'll be staining and varnishing, be sure to sand out all the marks with lighter grits of sandpaper.

- **Blower:** An electric (and quieter) version of the gas-powered leaf blowers that landscaping crews use. Some electric blowers also have a reverse feature and act as vacuums (such as Makita's). Blowers are inexpensive and they're great for blowing yard debris, sawdust, cobwebs from the garage—even

YOU'LL THANK YOURSELF LATER

Buy tools that fit your hands! An uncomfortable tool may change your mind about doing the job! A power tool should make your job easier. That said, I heartily recommend a Makita orbital finishing sander. It's inexpensive and doesn't vibrate as much as less expensive sanders.

dust and gum wrappers from the nooks and crannies of your car! If you're desperate, a blower may be the perfect tool to clean your kids' rooms! If you've been doing a lot of sanding or other dirty work, before you go back into the house, put on your ear protectors and blow yourself off. A blower is terrific for cleaning yourself up when you're covered with sawdust.

Rent or Borrow, Return Tomorrow

Some jobs might require a tool you'll only use once. Even though it might be cool to have a chainsaw hanging up in the garage, just how often are you going to be trimming that elm tree in the back yard? If it's tall, probably not at all! And you'll have to have an otherwise unnecessary garage sale to get rid of that chainsaw and all the other tools you don't use.

Some rent or borrow tools might include:

- Belt sander
- Disc sander
- Circular saw
- Jigsaw
- Table saw
- Floor sanders
- Chainsaw
- Nailing gun
- Rototiller (a popular garden tiller)

This list could go on forever, too! A cabinetmaker, for instance, can always find another tool to add to the shop. For your purposes, these tools, and others, might be needed for those once-in-a-blue-moon jobs, so don't add these to your birthday wish list!

- **Belt sander:** A sander using a continuous belt of sandpaper; good for sanding narrow surfaces. Bigger belt sanders can hold larger sized sanding belts. The larger the belt, the heavier the sander, so be sure you can handle it before you rent or borrow it.

- **Disc sanders:** These sanders use a round sanding disc and spin at very high speeds! Like other sanders, they come in different sizes according to the size of the sanding disc. They are good for grinding and sanding larger flat areas, but things can get out of hand quickly if you're not careful with them. Practice first on an old piece of wood or you could wind up with an even bigger project than you started with!

- **Circular saw:** The most common electric saw. Used for freehand cutting, mainly of framing lumber and plywood. For occasional use, an inexpensive saw will do. For one-time heavy duty use, rent a worm-drive circular saw.

- **Jigsaw:** Small electrical saw with a reciprocating (in-and-out) blade for intricate cutting. The term jigsaw puzzle tells it all!

If you're feeling uneasy about using a power saw, first practice on some scrap wood. Mutilate it with zeal until you're comfortable with the tool. Consider it a quick, cheap apprenticeship.

The Lazy Way

Table saw: This tool has a saw motor and blade mounted on a steel table. It's used for cutting longer lengths of trim and plywood. Table saws can be very dangerous around inexperienced users!

Floor sanders: Used for sanding wood floors. The larger of the two sanders is a drum sander, a machine about the size of a lawnmower, but much heavier. It takes a large sheet of sandpaper that is secured around the drum on the bottom of the sander. Its companion is an edger, a specialized disc sander for sanding the floor area near the baseboards. Both of these sanders spin at very high speeds and can gouge a floor in seconds if you don't know how to use them.

Chainsaw: Loud, effective—even lethal—chainsaws can be powered by either gasoline or electricity. The electric models start with the pull of the trigger— no cords to pull. It doesn't get any easier than that! For most trimming purposes, a small chainsaw is all you need. If you've got a large tree to take down, hire a licensed tree service.

Nailing gun: Only worth renting if you have a lot of nailing to do. Nailing guns can be used for framing, siding, and finish work—all of which is way beyond normal maintenance usage—but they're fun tools to use.

Rototiller: For all you green thumb types. These machines will cultivate the toughest patches of dirt

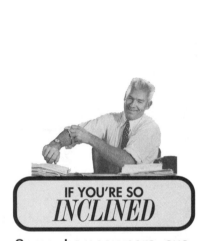

in just minutes and are well worth renting. A quick and painless alternative to a shovel and blisters! Rototiller is the trademarked name of a popular garden tiller.

Once-in-a-Blue-Moon Tools

Maybe you're borderline lazy, and straddle the fence between two distinct worlds. On one side is the land of leisure and hammocks, trashy beach novels, and a yellowing list of projects you keep meaning to get back to. On the other is the land of people who inherited the do-it-yourself-at-all-costs gene. They mill their own wood, blow their own window glass, and think of roofing as a recreational activity. Although you know you belong in the world of ease, you can't help but have grudging admiration for the worker bees on the other side. You like to visit their land every once in a while, as long as you can get back over the fence when you want to.

When the urge to do-it-yourself comes upon you, you may need one of the once-in-a-blue-moon tools on this list:

- Plumber's snake
- Reciprocating saw
- Electric plane
- Router
- Tile saw
- Chisels
- Pair of heavy duty extension ladders with plank

YOU'LL THANK YOURSELF LATER

Wrap your shovel and rake handles with foam pipe insulation. The tools will be more comfortable to use, won't slip out of your hands, and will prevent splinters and blisters. (It also creates a nice cushion for behind your head when you decide to take a ten-minute snooze.)

If you lose the protective covers or packaging that came with your saw blades, stick them in a block of styrofoam packing material. You can also use wall mounted magnetic knife holders.

Most of these tools should be rented, unless you have dreams of changing your life and becoming a contractor! Who needs that dumb corner office, paid medical, and yearly vacation when you can be out in the rain adding a dormer to your former colleague's house?

What once-in-a-blue-moon tools are for:

- **Plumber's snake:** Not the small, manual one, but a motorized metal python that will clean out your sewer lines should you decide to do it yourself instead of calling Rotomaniacs.

- **Reciprocal saw:** This resembles an electric carving knife; the straight, narrow blade moves in and out, making it ideal for cutting through wallboard and plaster. Some contractors prefer a small, electric chain saw for cutting through plaster and lath, but a reciprocal saw will certainly do the trick. In a pinch, you can use it on the Thanksgiving turkey or other large cuts of meat (clean the blade first, however). Surprise your relatives with your skill, and they may never ask you over for a holiday meal again.

- **Electric plane:** No, it's not a lightweight airplane attached to a very long cord. A hand plane is used by a finish carpenter to smooth, shape, and trim wood. An electric plane does the same thing, but much faster, making it ideal—in the right hands-for trimming long pieces of wood or for fitting doors. These are dangerous tools! The rotating blade on the underside of the plane has no guard on it. Practice on a piece of scrap lumber before you try it on your front door.

- **Router:** This tool makes those fancy designs you see on some trim and furniture. A million different attachments are available which attach to a revolving spindle on the end of the router motor. As they turn, they cut a pattern into the wood, and even work on metal. More for a cabinet maker but, who knows, you may decide to build your next dresser yourself.

- **Tile saw:** For cutting ceramic tile and marble (for all you bathroom and kitchen remodelers). This is a messy tool because it shoots water as the blade turns. If you're smart you'll do your cutting outside.

- **Wood chisels:** Good chisels make some wood fitting jobs a snap by accurately shaping wood for joinery (joining pieces of wood). Your wood chisels won't last long if you use them for such unjoinery-type purposes as chipping away at excess mortar on a brick wall or scraping rust off a lawnmower blade. Keep your chisels sharp and their tips protected.

- **Heavy duty extension ladders and a plank:** Ladders are sold in grades, not unlike beef, diamonds, and purebred dogs. Most homeowner ladders are light weight—which makes them a lot easier to use, but not as strong as a contractor would like. If you expect to spend a lot of time on extension ladders, rent a pair of commercial-grade ladders and an extension plank. The plank gives you a walkway between the ladders and speeds up your work. Warning: you can be seriously injured if you fall off a plank, so you should rent a safety harness and

IF YOU'RE SO INCLINED

Some friends and neighbors have small tool banks. They chip in on specialized tools so they'll be there when they're needed. If you can get the right group together, it's a good way to save cash.

rope to secure yourself. Commercial-grade ladders are heavier than homeowner grade, so have an extra body around to help you set them up.

There are always more tools to buy, rent, and borrow. They'll be waiting for you the next time you get the home repair urge—unless you fight it with a snack and a heavy-duty nap.

Better Safe Than Sorry

It's pretty hard to hurt yourself with a pair of pliers. They might slip and cut a finger, but a slip with an electric saw and you can cut a finger off! Even experienced workers are injured with power tools. Power tools turn burdensome jobs into manageable tasks, but you must be respectful of the tool and the danger it poses. Observe safety precautions. Wear eye and ear protection, including:

- Ear plugs or protective ear muffs
- Plastic safety glasses
- Dust masks

Never walk away and leave tools plugged in, especially around children! Saws come with safety guards, and it's tempting to remove them. Don't! Relax, take your time, and stay vigilant. Your job will be more manageable and you'll stay in one piece!

Now that you've assembled all your tools, put them away and forget about your chores for a day! You can do the job anytime, so relax, have a cup of tea, and get back to it later.

The Lazy Way

Getting Time on Your Side

	The Old Way	The Lazy Way
Drilling a 4-inch hole	5–10 minutes	1 minute
Cutting plywood sheet	10 minutes	1 minute
Sweeping driveway	15 minutes	1 minute
Cutting down a cherry tree (à la George Washington)	All morning	Less time than making toast
Digging up the garden for spring planting	Forever, since you'll never finish it with a shovel	1 hour
Explaining to your spouse why the bathroom you tore up still isn't tiled, since you decided to do it yourself instead of hiring a contractor	You'll always be explaining it	Nothing to explain; you never rented a tile saw, but called Mr. Tile instead

Part 2

The Lazy Homeowner's Shrewd Shortcuts

Are You Too Lazy to Read "Lazy Homeowner's Shrewd Shortcuts"?

1 You already think you're too hip for this world. ☐ yes ☐ no

2 Your idea of a shortcut is to skip this section altogether. ☐ yes ☐ no

3 The part about being a couch potato comes easily, but the cleaning part seems like too much of an existential stretch. ☐ yes ☐ no

Chapter three

Hip Organizing Tips

It's Around Here Someplace . . .

One of the ways we're distinguished from lower animals—in addition to participating in monster truck rallies and inventing I-can't-believe-it's-not-meat beef substitutes—is our use of tools. We use scissors, jack hammers, salad spinners, and hundreds of other implements to make our lives easier. The trouble is that the brain cells that control our ability to sort and store them are usually out on dates with synapses from the other side of our frontal lobes. By the time they stumble home, we can't find the hammer we used two days ago or the measuring tape we swore we put in the top kitchen drawer. Be wise, organize!

Think Ahead

Those wonderful tools you've bought to tighten a hinge or tap in a loose floor nail don't do you much good if you've hidden them away in the basement. Small repairs are easily put off if the screwdriver or hammer isn't close by. Put them off long enough and they can become big repairs!

The simple solution? A few extra tools, ready when you need them. You could keep a small set in:

1. The kitchen

2. An upstairs bedroom

3. The garage

   A small set would include:

- Hammer

- Multiple-bit screwdriver

- Roll of masking tape

- Pliers

Easier yet, buy one or two pre-packaged tool sets for about $15 each at a home center or hardware store. It's a small investment for a big convenience. These tools come in neat, folding plastic cases and are easily stored away.

Your main set of tools can be kept in one organized tool box, ready to be hauled in for larger jobs. The handy-type guys of the world often have grand work benches with Pegboard-mounted tools of every size and description. They grab what they need and pile them into wooden tool boxes they constructed years earlier in shop class and still keep varnished and clean. Sometimes they own beautiful, custom-made maple carriers with brass hinges and locks. They almost look like jewelry cases. You, on the other hand, aren't interested in keeping enough tools around to build a replica of Noah's ark or treating them like the Hope diamond. Tools are tools to you, and the less you have to use them, the better. Your spare time isn't spent at auction houses looking for things like a mid-18th century piano tuner's wrench. When all your hand tools are in one tool box:

1. It saves you trips back and forth from the job looking for tools you forgot.

2. Everything is in one place and less likely to get lost.

3. If storage space is tight, one tool box is easy to put away.

WHEN ONE TOOL BOX IS JUST A LITTLE TOO SMALL

Storage and access is everything, especially when a single tool box just won't do. Until tools come with feet or wheels and will come when called, they'll have to be put away and retrieved. Therefore, you'll find yourself crisscrossing Freudian roles playing mother and father to yourself as a child—you know, "Put your toys away or you won't have any to play with later." Mmmm. Just how would you punish yourself for not putting away the pipe wrench?

Storage for tools includes:

- A separate work room
- Various types of tool boxes
- A kitchen drawer

One Room, No View

If you have a basement or garage, it's a good idea to have a separate area to keep tools and work on house

YOU'LL THANK YOURSELF LATER

Saws and chisels have sharp edges. Keep them that way! Wrap each cutting edge with a protective guard. If one doesn't come with the tool, use a bent piece of thin cardboard held on with rubber bands.

Outlining your tools on Pegboard is a great way to help your kids learn to return tools. Show them the tool's outline and teach them to put it back on the right hooks. Most kids learn this in nursery school, so it's good reinforcement!

and hobby projects. This room should have:

- A workbench
- Overhead lighting
- An electrical outlet
- Pegboard, hooks, and shelves

Complete workbenches ready for assembly and use can be purchased at some home improvement centers. They're pretty convenient for small spaces and most household projects. If you prefer to build your own, inquire about any free building plans your home center may have available. If you've got the room, build a large work bench, at least 8-feet long. This is a standard length for a lot of dimensional lumber, so you'll have less cutting to do.

Pegboard is that popular hard fiberboard material sold in sheets. Each sheet is perforated with about a million holes into which special metal hooks are inserted to hold your tools. You can paint Pegboard, by the way, if its homey brown color doesn't quite go with your workroom motif. If you use Pegboard:

- Buy plenty of hooks.
- Group your tools by type.
- Hang the tool and draw an outline around it.

If your collection of tools grows, you may need plenty of display space. Take a wide felt marker or fingernail polish and trace onto the Pegboard and around the tool to form an outline. This makes finding its place on the wall effortless!

On the Move

Tool boxes come in all sizes and shapes including:

- Large, rolling mechanic's tool box
- Metal or plastic tool boxes
- Open wooden tote-type boxes
- Wooden tool chests

Mechanics like to lock up their tools every night; they want everything in the same place the next day. There's a reason service stations post those, "We Do Not Loan Tools, Not Even to Our Mothers" signs in their windows. You won't need anything this size unless you're repairing a '65 MGB, in which case, your rolling tool box will become part of your permanent garage decor (until you get rid of the MGB, anyway). Wooden tool chests can usually be found in your grandfather's workshop, along with tools you can't even identify. Don't ask, unless you're prepared for a long lecture on the history of coping saws.

For most home purposes, a metal or plastic tool box will do. If you haven't got room for a tool room in your house, this is the way to go.

The Small Stuff

As a homeowner, over time you'll start accumulating screws, nails, nuts, bolts, hinges, and bags full of odds and ends from all your trips to the hardware store. How do you know what's what without opening a shelf full of bags?

A COMPLETE WASTE OF TIME

The 3 Worst Ways to Store Small Stuff

1. Mix everything together in a shoe box.

2. Throw everything in the kitchen junk drawer.

3. Not separate specialty items, like those metric bolts that came with your Italian bicycle.

You can organize these items in:

- Clear glass jars
- Small sets of plastic drawers
- Plastic storage containers with dividers

Glass jars are sensible and cheap, but you'll need a shelf to store them on. Metal cabinets with small plastic drawers are sold at home improvement centers and general merchandise stores for this very purpose: storing small, miscellaneous items. Hobbyists use them to store beads, buttons, and small electronic components. If space is at a premium, buy some tough, flat plastic containers with built-in dividers. These are perfect for those pesky, need-them-once-in-a while items that you can never find because they're always buried in bags.

The Big Stuff

Power tools have kind of macho personalities and demand their own space. The top-of-the-line models even come with their own metal carrying cases. Try and get one of those past an airport metal detector. You can build shelves for them, or do it the easy way: go to a garage sale! Look for:

- An old dresser
- Used luggage
- An old buffet

Sometimes thrift stores, such as the Salvation Army, are even better places to look for these items. You want them cheap! Old luggage is the perfect way to carry power tools to the job site and store them at home too. An old dresser that's seen better days offers instant storage—and you don't have to build anything! One bicycle shop owner in the metropolis of Kent, Washington, stored a lot of small tools in two turn-of-the-century oak dressers which had been painted pink. It drove his customers nuts; they were always trying to buy them from him so they could strip and restore them. He wouldn't budge; Leonard knew cheap storage when he saw it.

HASSLE-FREE HELPERS: BORROW OR RENT AND FORGET ABOUT IT

Sometimes the best way to get organized is to let someone else bear the burden and expense of owning and maintaining tools, especially if it's something you rarely use, like that bread maker you bought six months ago and still haven't taken out of the box. This is where the rental business comes in. If a rental price is low enough, especially if it's for one-time use, consider renting instead of buying.

Renting Tools

Collecting tools doesn't seem to be anywhere near the problem for women as it is for men. Maybe 10,000 years ago women understood that it was more important to gather and store nuts and berries, while their hubbies were adding more stone mallets to their tool collections.

Most power tools can be rented, as can many hand tools. As is not the case with bowling shoes, you really won't care who used them before you! A little

QUICK ⬤ PAINLESS

Floor sanders, Rototillers, professional table saws—any specialized heavy equipment for one-time jobs—should always be rented. Purchase rental insurance against accidental damage. Easiest yet: if you don't have a truck, pay the rental company to do the pickup and delivery!

YOU'LL THANK YOURSELF LATER

Check out rental costs and availability at more than one facility. Some stores offer special rates for rentals picked up at closing time on Saturday night and returned on Monday morning. Multi-day rentals may be less expensive per day than one-day rentals.

consideration and some economics will help you determine whether renting is the way for you.

To figure out if you should rent, you need to consider the:

- Purchase price of the equipment vs. the rental cost.

- Expected frequency of usage.

- Long-term use.

This strategy holds true for smaller tools as well, right down to sledge hammers, if the rental price is right. Consider:

- Is this a one-time job?

- Can this tool be used for other jobs?

- Is this a high-maintenance tool?

Borrowing Tools

It's always easier to borrow a neighbor's or friend's tools than to troop off to a rental outlet. This is probably an okay strategy for manual tools like hammers and rakes and screw drivers, but borrowing power tools is another arena altogether. If you're going to borrow power tools:

- Be on good terms with the lender.

- Establish an understanding of responsibility if the tool breaks.

- Be prepared to pay for a replacement.

Friendships and neighborhood cordiality can become very strained if you borrow someone's 25-year-old-don't-build-'em-like-they-use-to drill and return it out of order because you didn't know a smoking motor was a signal to stop drilling. Just because someone is willing to loan you a tool doesn't necessarily mean it's a good idea. So be sure you know what you're getting into.

Renting is incredibly easy. You simply need to:

- Call and confirm that the tool or item you want is in stock.
- Present a driver's license for identification.
- Leave a credit card slip or check for a deposit.
- Pick up extra saw blades, drill bits, sandpaper, etc. for your chosen tool. You can always return unused items for a refund.
- Return it at the agreed upon time or, as a courtesy, inform the rental store if you need more time.

Whether you borrow or rent it, if you are unfamiliar with how a tool operates:

- Get some instructions.
- Ask the clerk to test any power tool or machine to see if it's functioning before you leave the shop.
- Don't rent any tool you think is unsafe.

Use and Abuse

Rental tools are like rental cars: you won't be quite as careful with them as you would if you owned them. This is not a license to abuse, but a kind of permission to utilize their full potential. The beauty of renting is that you can borrow nicer tools than you would normally be willing to buy, and that will cut down your work time and effort.

You survived the job, the tools have been returned—hooray for you! Stop off at the bakery on the way home from the rental shop and stuff yourself with a couple of cream-puffs.

The Lazy Way

If a rented tool breaks or is no longer working properly, you should:

▪ Stop using it immediately.

▪ Look for the problem.

▪ Return it for a refund or exchange.

Power tools wear out, and rental shops understand this. It may go out the door running just fine, but in your hands the motor revolves around just one too many times and then decides to stop working. It isn't your fault. If you didn't damage it intentionally, you won't be charged. And the rental time will be adjusted.

When your job is completed, return the tool:

▪ Clean and wiped down.

▪ With all cords neatly wrapped.

▪ With your original contract.

There was an article in the *Wall Street Journal* describing guys (apparently there still aren't a lot of women tool addicts) who'd decided that, now that they'd made lots of money in the stock market, what they really wanted was a fully functioning woodworking shop in the garage. The fact that few of them knew one end of a joiner from another didn't stop them from spending thousands—and thousands—of dollars on top-of-the-line tools. Their tool-buying outings did accomplish something—the contractors they ran into at the local hardware store had a good laugh.

Getting Time on Your Side

	The Old Way	The Lazy Way
Finding the hammer you thought you left in the garage	Forget it; faster to buy a new one	2 minutes
Running down to the basement for a screw-driver because you don't have an extra one in the kitchen	10 minutes if you have to find it down there	30 seconds if you're slow
Tracking down the guy who borrowed your hammer and didn't sign it out	Good luck, Sherlock	A phonecall away
Finding some 3-inch sheetrock screws	Empty out every drawer and dig	Go to the 3-inch sheetrock screw jar
Pegboard vs. a big cardboard box full of tools	Start digging again	20 seconds flat to find any tool
Building a workbench vs. buying one	Are you kidding?	1 trip to the store

Chapter

four

Quick Fixes

We're surrounded by so many lists that we need a list just to keep the other ones in order! A small note pad can keep your maintenance on track and trouble-free. Put it next to your phone and keep track of:

- Small repair jobs that come up.
- Lists of materials needed.
- Contractors to call.

Chapter 18 tells how to devise a calendar of regular maintenance so you can get through it quickly without skipping anything. Sometimes other problems come up—like a torn vinyl floor tile in the kitchen or a leaky faucet—and a written reminder helps keep the jobs from getting out of hand. A quick note, a list of what to buy, and you're halfway there! If it's too big of a job—like a garage door opener that's slowly dying—you'll know to call a contractor and have it repaired.

I'LL NEED THAT IN WRITING

Train all the adults and older kids in your house to keep track of these things and write them down. Make it clear that this

QUICK 🔘 PAINLESS

Try having a family Job Jar. Everyone draws a slip of paper with a maintenance chore on it. This doesn't work unless you sprinkle a few surprises in with the jobs. "Skip a chore" and "Go to the movies while dad works" are good ones.

isn't a chore list for them—which of course it is. You'll just have to figure out some creative way to get everyone not only to act against their own best interest by finding work to do, but then cheerfully do it. Figure this out and your house maintenance won't be all that complicated.

When it comes to maintenance, treat your house like it belongs to someone else and you're a paid manager. You'd be surprised what a change in perspective can do for you! No, it doesn't mean you can start padding the expense account. J.P. Getty, one of America's first certified billionaires (whose picture is next to the word "cheapskate" in the dictionary), took care of his old Cadillac as if he were the chauffeur. He said he did it because no one could care enough to do a better job; he was right; the car lasted for many years. If you care about your house, it'll stay in good shape for a long time. I'd hold off treating the kids like employees, though. They'd probably strike for higher wages or turn you in for violating child labor laws.

DIVIDE AND CONQUER

In America, perception is everything. We can spend three hours doing two weeks worth of washing all at once, or spread it out and do one load at a time. It's nice to end up with more clean clothes when we need them, but it isn't necessarily faster to do all the laundry at once. Is it worth sticking ourselves with hours on end of unrelieved drudgery? Breaking up a task into small pieces makes it much less of a hassle. This does not mean tossing your socks in the sink with the breakfast dishes.

The Great Outdoors

Summer rolls around and you want to spend some time in the great outdoors—your yard! Do two things at once, and cut your work down. When you're washing your car, you can:

- Rinse down a side of the house.
- Wash a few windows.
- Water some plants.
- Rinse the driveway and walks.

Barbecuing for the crew? Take 10 minutes while the chicken is cooking and:

- Pull weeds from one flower bed.
- Check for burned-out yard lights.
- Fertilize some plants.

These are quick, manageable jobs, not big, drawn out labors. Walk around the yard and pull a few weeds every evening. If your yard's in good shape, you'll have little to do over the weekend!

Those Autumn Leaves

As fall approaches, you may not be spending as much leisure time in your yard—unless you live in someplace fun like Hawaii! For all you readers at the South Pole, I guess leisure time outdoors means a quick dash out to the porch to pick up the daily paper. For everyone else, it's easy to get ready for winter. While you're out raking the leaves:

IF YOU'RE SO
INCLINED

Speaking of weeds, an old steak knife makes a great gardening tool. Sharpen the edge and use it to cut a weed at its roots, and dig it out. It's simple, and it makes good use of an old knife.

- Start installing a few storm windows.
- Do any final paint touch-up.
- Clean one gutter a week.
- Trim any wayward bushes (if seasonally appropriate).
- Plant spring bulbs.

Break it down! Plant 200 tulip bulbs in one morning and you might think twice about ever dealing with these glorified onions again. Spread the task out while the weather is still good, and take your time. Note: Death Valley residents can ignore the above list.

Changing of the Guard

As winter approaches, you can store those rakes and hoes away—good riddance. The next time you're in the garage:

- Wipe a few of your yard tools with a rag and spray cleaner.
- Spray with silicone or WD-40 when dry.
- Rub paraffin on your snow shovels (makes shoveling easier).

A few trips to the garage and you're done! Do this when you're taking the garbage out and soon your tools will be tucked away for the winter.

While you're out there:
- Wipe down and cover the yard furniture.
- Store the bicycles.
- Pack up the golf clubs.
- Inspect your skis for the coming season.

YOU'LL THANK YOURSELF LATER

You can still touch up paint late into the fall. Just follow the directions on the can. Winter weather is rough on paint. Keep it touched up and repaired, and you can put off that big paint job a while longer!

- Drain and turn off the outside faucets and store hoses.

- Don't let chores pile up! Ignore some of them—like cleaning your gutters—and you'll have a huge job later! Take a simple and organized approach and they won't be burdensome at all!

Wipe Your Feet!

What's the simplest way to cut down on floor cleaning and maintenance?

- Install large door mats at all entryways to your house.

- Remove your shoes at the door.

Shoes carry dirt and grit, and then conveniently distribute it all over your rugs, carpet, and hardwood floors. Take them off and wear house slippers, and your floors will be in great shape! If it's a problem with guests, door mats are the next best thing.

We could learn a thing or two from some other cultures—in addition to all those fun ways the French prepare sauces. In Japanese homes, it's traditional to remove your street shoes at the door and slip on appropriate indoor footwear. It's a habit worth considering—especially if you can get your children to adopt it at an early age.

Shopping List

The next time you are at your favorite icon to American commerce, the warehouse store, buy large containers of:

A COMPLETE WASTE OF TIME

The 3 Worst Ways to Winterize

1. Ignore the gutters—and almost guarantee they'll fill with water that won't drain properly.

2. Leave the garden hoses outside, and still attached to the faucets.

3. Skip yearly furnace maintenance.

- Baking soda
- Vinegar
- Bleach

These are the big three for housecleaning and odor removal, and keeping your life simple! What can they do?

Pour a generous amount of bleach down a really smelly disposal; rinse with hot water after it sits for three hours.

Sprinkle one-half a box of baking soda into a toilet tank once a month; let it sit overnight and it will clean both the tank and the bowl. It won't replace your normal ritual of scrubbing the bowl, but a few hours of baking soda can really help.

Freshen carpet by sprinkling it with baking soda—using a flour sifter—and vacuuming 30 minutes later. Ask the dog to move if she's lying in her favorite spot, unless you want to freshen her up at the same time. If she doesn't mind being vacuumed, it just might work.

Clean fats and soap buildup from your kitchen drain by pouring in a generous amount of baking soda, followed by a liberal dose of vinegar. The chemical reaction neutralizes the fats, and clears the drain. Vinegar is also a great rinsing agent. Mix it with rinse water to mop up soap residue after you wash your floors.

Let the big three do their job and you have almost nothing to do!

QUICK n PAINLESS

Some people wisely put an open box of baking soda in their refrigerators each month to absorb odors. Do this and then pour the month-old box into your toilets. It does two jobs for the price of one!

Do We Have Plans for You!

The best time to plan large jobs, like repainting rooms or changing carpeting, is months in advance when you have no deadlines. This gives you time to:

- Consider colors.
- Pick out materials.
- Pick out designs.
- Choose appliances.

How do you make this easy? Simple. The next time you're shopping:

- Stop at a paint store and pick up color samples.
- Check out wallpaper designs.
- Browse through carpet samples.
- Compare different appliances.

Do the legwork ahead of time and you'll be ready to go when it's time to take on the project. Some people plan big projects for years. One couple saved up ideas for redoing kitchens from *Sunset Magazine* and other places until they finally went ahead and did it. They'd avoided a lot of hassles by deciding what they liked long before the work began. Of course, *Sunset* featured them and the new kitchen prominently in a subsequent issue.

Working the Room

You're a homeowner. When the furnace stops running on Christmas Eve, you can't depend on Mom to come and make things right. (Okay, you can if she owns Big Momma's Heating and Cooling Service and she works

You can plan a project, such as redoing your kitchen, well in advance by clipping ideas from magazines. It avoids a lot of hassles if you decide what you want long before the work begins.

holidays.) Forget the family discount; she still remembers the time she had to fix it on Thanksgiving. She remains unconvinced to this day that that's not the reason you invited her over for dinner. Otherwise, you need a list of reliable contractors—and I stress the word reliable. There are plenty of them around and they tend to stay busy. How do you find them? Ask everyone! And you can do it any time! Everyone includes:

- Your neighbors
- Co-workers
- Dentist and doctor
- Other contractors

Your neighbors may have good leads to local contractors they've found reliable. Co-workers, especially upper management, can be a great resource. Higher-paid individuals may be more particular—read demanding—about who works on their homes. Same with your dentist and doctor. Contractors have high standards—they often depend on their peers to get their own work finished—and can be a good resource for referrals.

When I was growing up, my father did a lot of home repairs but, since he was a physician, his time was limited. How did he find contractors? He would call some of his former patients. My mother never knew who to expect when he'd say, "A patient of mine is going to be by to _____ (fill in the blank)." Being a patient, apparently, was a sufficient qualification for doing work on our home. Usually, things turned out all right, but then

YOU'LL THANK YOURSELF LATER

You found a competent, reliable plumber? Great! That business card is your ticket to guaranteed running water for life. Be a good customer, pay on time, and you'll be rewarded over and over—like every time you take a shower.

there was the house painter who camped out for most of the summer . . .

Get a list going at your leisure and you'll have people to call when you need them! When you find good people, be sure to spread their names around. Contractors depend to a great extent on word-of-mouth referrals for their business.

Associate and Mitigate

You can't very well drop everything between, say, dinnertime and bedtime and go off to paint a side of your house. Well, maybe you can if you have a 4-foot wide paintbrush. But you can work regular maintenance around other chores. When you pay your monthly bills, you can also:

- Change a furnace filter.
- Check your smoke detectors.
- Clean the washable filter in your range hood.

Tie one task in with another and you'll feel like you're getting two things done at once.

IF YOU'RE SO
INCLINED

If you have a large job to do, say major landscaping, you might consider hiring a professional for a day to give you some lessons. A contractor may be willing to do this as long as you don't demand any trade secrets!

Getting Time on Your Side

	The Old Way	The Lazy Way
Finding a contractor you like in the Yellow Pages vs. a recommendation	Start dialing	One call away
Cleaning the leaves from the gutters in October vs. chipping the ice out in January	Wear your gloves	2–4 hours
Pulling a few weeds nightly vs. once a month	Grab your machete	10 minutes
Maintaining a chore list vs. trying to remember what needs to be done	Uh, oh, did we fix that leak yet?	A few minutes a week
Exterior paint touch-ups vs. major repainting	Hope your summer is free	1–2 hours in the fall
Cleaning the garage bit by bit in the early fall vs. waiting until the first snow	Your car will start better if it's left outside	20 minutes a week

five

The Couch Potato Quick Clean

Did you have a mom who nagged you to clean up after yourself? Chances are it wasn't just to build your character—she didn't want to clean up either!

You're an adult now and things haven't changed. You still have picking up to do and it's still not fun, especially after you've been cleaning out the gutters or painting a closet. At that point, who wouldn't want to walk away from it and let somebody else deal with it? You could try calling the Environmental Protection Agency to get your home put on the Super Fund clean-up list, but they might put you out on the street for a few years until they can get to those dust bunnies.

If you have to clean up, be smart and make it easier on yourself.

PLASTIC—THE GREAT PREVENTER

Plastic is one of the finest by-products ever produced from a barrel of oil. We build cars with plastic, eat tortilla chips out of

plastic bags, and carry not a few pieces of it in our wallets. And for clean up, you can't beat it.

Tear It and Toss It

Plastic is sold in rolls of varying sizes and thickness. The sheets that come pre-cut and packaged are really pretty useless. Spend a few extra dollars and buy plastic that's at least 3mm (millimeters) thick. You even have a choice between black plastic and clear. If a whole roll is more than you need, buy it in black, and you can use it for Halloween decorations. You can open one up and zip off the size piece you need with a utility knife in seconds. It can be used for just about anything. To cut your clean-up time down, use plastic when you:

- Paint
- Create debris
- Repair walls
- Need a catch-all

Hmm, That Color Isn't Quite Right . . .

Professional painters normally use heavy drop cloths to protect floors and furniture when they paint. These are very thick, and specially made to keep spattered paint on top of the cloth without soaking through to the surface beneath it. Do you want a pile of these hanging around your garage for the occasional paint job? Good luck washing them—these things don't lend themselves to normal-sized washing machines. Who wants all that gunk floating around in the washer anyway? And don't think the laundromat will roll out the welcome mat for you, either. Washing drop cloths ends up being a stealth mission in the dark of night when the chief laundress/launderer isn't around. If you're doing the job yourself, plastic is a much simpler solution. If you're doing the job yourself, plastic is a much simpler solution.

Whether in large jobs or small, the laws of nature dictate that paint must drip or spatter onto the floor or any unprotected surface—including the painter! Cover your work area completely with a sheet of plastic. At the end of the job, roll it up and toss it in the trash. That's as easy as it gets!

Don't forget to cover yourself up, too (but not with plastic—remember all those childhood warnings about suffocation?). Paint stores sell disposable paper suits that can be used over and over again. They cost only a few dollars and are a great investment. If you want to get into a popular movie at the local mall and there's a really long line, you can always print the words "Nuclear Waste Disposal" on the back, wear a respirator, and carry a clipboard. You should be able to get any seat you want.

Paint stores often give away painter's caps or sell them cheap. Wear one, or your hair could end up making an unintentional fashion statement. May as well pick up some inexpensive cotton work gloves while you're at it. They're thin enough to allow flexible work, like painting, while being some protection against grime and stains.

The easiest cleanup is the cleanup you avoided. Wipe those shoes, keep a small vacuum cleaner nearby when you do a messy project, and work carefully. That's the simple way to stay clean.

Debris Deep Six

When landscapers mow lawns and clean away leaves, they often dump everything onto large pieces of canvas or other heavy cloth and drag them away to their trucks. You won't catch them filling one plastic trash bag after another until they have a small mountain of them. Why should you? When you have a lot of yard waste to dispose of, take the low road. All you'll need is:

- Roll of plastic
- Knife
- Duct tape

Cut a large sheet of plastic and lay it out near your work area. Use a rake to pile on your spring or fall yard waste—leaves, grass, twigs, etc. When you have a good sized pile, pull the four corners of the plastic together over it. Wrap your roll of duct tape around it a few times to secure it, and it's ready to be tossed on a truck. This is a lot faster than filling plastic bags! Better yet—if you want to spend the money—buy a mulching lawn mower. It'll grind up your grass and leaves, and spread them right back onto the lawn as compost. No bagging, no disposal—and great for your lawn.

The other choice is to actually build a compost pile, but unless you're into organic gardening, that's a lot of work. Besides, you still have to get all the leaves and debris into the compost bin. If your municipality does their own recycling and composting, cheerfully get rid of the stuff by giving it to them.

YOU'LL THANK YOURSELF LATER

Plastic by the roll is cheap. The price is usually better at a lumber store or home center than at a hardware store. Keep a couple of rolls around for those unexpected jobs.

Mastering Plastering

Large job or small, wall repair generally produces some dust and it all falls straight down. Down might be your new carpet or your oak floors. Who wants that?

Cover your work area with a sheet of plastic and let it catch everything: dust, wet plaster, Spackle, any old material you have to dig out. Roll it up and give it your best slam dunk into the trash can. This does not work if your entire house is being demolished for a new condominium development—that stuff will just have to be trucked away.

Catch Me If You Can

Old houses are full of surprises. You may have to tear out part of a shingled wall or some bathroom tile. Plastic is a great catch-all for all the discarded bits and pieces of yesteryear. Take the same approach you would with excess yard debris: lay a piece of plastic down, toss the debris on top, and wrap it up like a holiday present for the landfill. No messing around with bags or empty wine boxes (they're especially fun when the bottoms drop out). The whole point is to get the job over with and forget you ever had to do it. Memories of filling plastic trash bags with dust pan after dust pan of chopped-up house are something you can do without.

LIFE IN A VACUUM

Original electric vacuum cleaners were pretty wretched affairs. Bulky and heavy, they weren't all that great at cleaning. As with a lot of technology, new vacuum

YOU'LL THANK YOURSELF LATER

The easiest cleanup is the cleanup you avoided. Wipe those shoes, keep a small vacuum cleaner nearby when you do a messy project, and work carefully. That's the lazy way to keep things clean.

cleaners are greatly advanced and relatively inexpensive. The right vacuum will cut your clean-up time to nothing flat!

Eureka!

Normally, a Shopvac is used by tradespeople for cleaning up sawdust and small work debris from carpentry projects. Shopvacs suck everything into a large metal or plastic canister instead of into vacuum cleaner bags. Large Shopvacs tend to be bulky and are overkill for most house jobs. Plus, they tend to shoot out an initial blast of exhaust dust when you first turn them on. Unless you want to add to your clean-up job, I don't recommend using a Shopvac in a relatively clean room.

Enter Eureka, an old name in the vacuum cleaner industry, and maker of the Mighty Mite vacuum cleaner. These are wonderful machines: compact, powerful—and they last forever. Take one of these lightweight vacuum cleaners around as you do your repairs, and cleaning up will be child's play. Then go call your mother and tell her that you've reformed, and might even go over and clean up your old room. If she calmly reminds you that she and your father moved out of that house 10 years ago, just remind her that it's the thought that counts, tardy as it may be.

Well, Blow Me Down

Small electric blowers are a vacuum cleaner's other half. They are perfect for:

- Blowing cobwebs and dust out of garages, basements, and attics.

- Cleaning off driveways and sidewalks.
- Removing sawdust from outdoor carpentry projects.
- Blowing dust off yourself.
- Intimidating the pesky neighborhood dog when he wanders into your yard

Did you ever try to clean up a few years' worth of dust in a garage full of shelves and nooks and crannies? A blower will do it in minutes—no elbow grease required!

Dusty walks or driveway? Don't fuss, raise some dust and blow it off in minutes.

Sawdust is organic and should break down in your yard or garden. If you've been sawing outdoors, a blower will clear the work space in a jiffy; no broom required!

Maybe you're covered with dust from your project, especially if you've been sanding. Don't track it into the house (you'll have to clean it up later). While you're still wearing your ear and eye protection, blow yourself off and leave the dust outside where it belongs!

Blowers are addictive—well, for guys, anyway. You'll probably need a 100-foot extension cord to snake around the house and yard, whisking away every loose, small object in sight.

Squeaky Clean

Have you finished cleaning out that clogged sink? How about scooping out the fireplace ashes? Leave a few smudges and fingerprints around the house? A few squirts of Windex or another glass cleaner followed by a

QUICK n PAINLESS

Personal testimonial: I used a Mighty Mite for years! It pulled up paint chips, small chunks of plaster, nails, screws—you name it. I even emptied and reused one bag for over a year! No doubt Eureka wouldn't recommend any of these practices, but I sure had more time to relax.

swipe with a paper towel and no one will ever know you were there. Despite the name, spray bottles of glass cleaner are multi-purpose and can clean just about anything. They're perfect for the quick clean after a job around the house. Your significant other will be very impressed with your clean work habits! Watch out! It may give her or him ideas about expanding your housekeeping duties.

QUICK ⬛ PAINLESS

Keep a roll of plastic, paper towels, and glass cleaner in a separate box or plastic tote so it will be easy to carry to a job location.

Getting Time on Your Side

	The Old Way	**The Lazy Way**
Sweeping sawdust	10 minutes	2 minutes
Bagging leaves	20 minutes	10 minutes
Cleaning sidewalks	15 minutes	5 minutes
Cleaning paint off yourself and your clothes after you re-coat the bedroom ceiling	Start scrubbing	Strip off the paper suit
Using a Eureka Mighty Mite to clean up the cat hair	20 minutes of hauling	Get rid of the cat: 5 minutes
Tracking debris through the house	A mess to clean up	Cut your clean-up in half
Cleaning up as you do the job vs. being a slob	Make clean-up a mountain to climb	No extra clean-up here!

View from a Hammock: Easy-as-Pie House Upkeep

Are You Too Lazy to Read "View from a Hammock"?

1 You've run out of paintings to cover the holes in your walls.
☐ yes ☐ no

2 The grass in your yard is so tall that your children play hide-and-seek in it. ☐ yes ☐ no

3 The water in your tub takes so long to drain out that new life forms are growing in it. ☐ yes ☐ no

The Anatomy of a House

Most of the time, we take our homes for granted. We expect the water to come flowing out of a tap on demand. Lights should go on with the flip of a switch and rain and snow should stay outside where they belong. Our homes put up with winds, summer heat, ice storms, lumbering dogs, and a million pounding footsteps from all of us. We expect them to carry on with a smile.

Unfortunately, houses like this exist only in novels. With a little knowledge, you could give your plot a happy ending.

All Houses Are Equal—Some Are Just More Equal Than Others

Our homes never heard of the Declaration of Independence. Citizens may be created equal (tell that to Donald Trump), but houses range from beach shacks to Silicon Valley–financed plantations. They also vary by age. A 19th century Victorian is a much different house than a brand new, the-paint's-still-drying suburban contemporary.

A house is like your child, without all the weird high school friends. But its behavior at the various stages of its life is the reverse of ours.

A new house behaves like a successful, grown adult offspring, still needing some love and affection, but getting by quite well for the most part. Your new place needs almost nothing done to it if the contractor did a good job.

An older home is similar to a teenager, challenging your anger management program by beginning to break things and get a little expensive. An older home will begin to need more attention.

If you have a really old home, say, more than 40 or 50 years of age—and especially turn-of-the-century charmers—then you have an infant on your hands: crying, cranky, and only content for brief periods of time before something else sets it off.

New houses are wonderful and are not without charm. There is very little maintenance other than regular seasonal chores. For busy people, new is often better, but a new house does not and can never feel the same as a really old house. If you own an older home with the charm and quaintness that would be prohibitive to duplicate today, the trade-off is that it will need more upkeep than a new house.

A middle-aged house could be 10, 20 or 30 years old, and its condition will depend partly on how much or little you use and/or abuse it. Lack of use won't turn back the hands of time; paint still fades and roofs age. The same maintenance strategy holds true for these houses as for much older ones: once it's brought up to newer standards, it's easier to maintain. It all depends on the condition of the house, the time and money you have to spend, and the kind of home you want to live in.

Your house will fit one of the following categories:

- New/Newer House (less than 15 years old)

- Older (10 to 50 years old)

- Old (older than 50 years)

These categories don't reflect a strict classification system, but they do represent some changes in construction practices and materials used over the years. When they reach about 15 years of age, appliances and water heaters—and sometimes roofs—decide to retire, and you know you're not in Kansas (i.e., a new house) anymore.

It Would Be Wood

Most of our homes are built of, or around, wood.

Certain framing basics remain true for all houses. Simply put, a house with wood framing is engineered to support a certain amount of weight and mass based on the framing configuration and the size of its framing members. The framing itself sits on a concrete foundation. The weight and size of the house determines the size and thickness of the foundation. Everything is based on local and national building codes that are enforced by building inspectors. When it's all tied together, it stays put, and so do you.

Probably, the most you'll ever interact with your house's framing is when you hang a picture on the wall.

IF YOU'RE SO
INCLINED

You can add touches to a new home—such as cove moldings along the ceiling and wider baseboards—to bring about an "older" feel to it. These don't have to be terribly expensive, and can give you the more lived-in feeling that comes with age.

(You know, when you try to hammer in a nail and it never hits anything solid. Soon you have 10 holes in the wall and you still can't hang your picture.)

If only to support your urge to decorate the walls, and provide assurance that your floor really will hold up a waterbed, here are some basics about framing:

- Joists run the length and width of the house and support the floors.

- Studs run vertically in walls and have plaster or wallboard attached to them.

- Rafters or trusses support the roof.

- Sheathing is installed on the exterior and is covered with the siding visible to you.

- Subflooring is nailed to the joists and is covered with wood flooring, carpet, vinyl, or tile.

You can almost bet that both joists and studs were installed 16 inches on center, which means that there is 16 inches from the center of one board to the center of the other. Knowing this will help you find a stud for hanging that picture or mirror. Once you've located one board, it's easy to find another.

There's a myth that, in the past, house construction was a great art and every worker was a craftsman. Where did this come from? If $50 could be cut from the cost of a $3,000-house and still meet the building specifications, don't you think that any builder in any period of history would take the money and run?

Costs and time have always been factors in construction and it's no different today. You could argue that the

QUICK n' PAINLESS

Go to your hardware store or home center and buy a battery-powered stud finder, which detects the location of studs under plaster and wallboard. These make picture hanging amazingly simple and less frustrating.

detailing work has suffered, but you get what you pay for. Throw enough money at it and you can have a perfect duplicate of a 1920s Tudor.

A new house today is built to a much tougher building code than our grandparents knew. Lead-based paint and lead plumbing fixtures have been outlawed. Electrical wiring is far safer. Seismic concerns are stressed in areas known for earthquakes. Heating and cooling systems are much more efficient. Still, a new house isn't perfect. It's only as good as the contractor who builds it and the materials it's built with.

Basements: Bottoms Up

In some parts of the country, basements are as unheard of as IRS thank-you notes. Besides being huge catch-alls for boxes of holiday ornaments, baby pictures, and old ice skates, basements usually contain the furnace, electrical box, and major plumbing. If you have an unfinished basement, the ceiling will show exposed wires, pipes, and heat ducts.

In a basement, you should check for:

- The presence of water, especially after a rain storm (this may indicate that you have drainage problems around the perimeter of the house).

- Insects, such as termites, or rodents, such as rats and mice. They'll leave sawdust, droppings, or maybe some dead companions behind.

- Moist or damp floors and walls.

A COMPLETE WASTE OF TIME

The 3 Worst Ways to Remodel a Basement

1. Cover up moisture problems in the walls or floors instead of repairing them.

2. Cover up an exposed ceiling/first floor before you've completed wiring or plumbing projects for which you'll need access.

3. Try to build in living space in a basement with a low ceiling (storage is fine).

Floors: Walking the Walk

Creaks and squeaks get our attention, but apart from that, unless the dog or cat runs across the floors with muddy paws, we hardly notice them. Floors get covered for comfort as well as aesthetics (who wants to walk across, or look at, raw plywood?). A floor will have at least two layers of material: a subfloor and a floor covering. The only one you'll ever have to worry about is the floor covering and how to maintain it. (See Chapter 15 for more.)

IF THESE WALLS COULD TALK

There are walls, and there are walls. Some are load-bearing, that is, if you remove one of them without supporting the section of the house it's holding up, you had better have the resilience of cartoon characters who jump right back up after cars run over them and anvils drop on their heads. Generally, if an interior wall runs perpendicular to the floor joists, you can figure it's a load-bearing wall. If you have any inclination to remove a wall, have it looked at first by a contractor, engineer, or architect.

Walls are almost always covered with either plaster or wallboard. Plaster is applied over wood lath, which holds the plaster in place as it dries. Lath is a latticework of thin boards nailed to the wall studs to form a framework for wet plaster. Before you ask, no, you can't hammer a nail into it and expect it to hold anything heavier than a lightweight picture. It's not meant for this. Try it, and your grandmother's antique mirror will end up on the floor!

IF YOU'RE SO INCLINED

Special hardware is available if you need to hang a medium-weight item and a wall stud isn't conveniently available. Ask your hardware store or home center clerk about molly bolts and toggle bolts for this purpose.

Plasterboard is a plaster-type material pressed into ready-to-hang sheets and hung with special nails or drywall screws. It comes in different thicknesses depending on the building requirements (a fire rating, for instance). It is the most common wall building material for new residential use. Hanging and finishing wallboard or drywall is a lot tougher than it looks!

Bathrooms and Kitchens: Clearing the Air

Bathroom and kitchen ventilation is a big deal. You want the steam and moisture out pronto to prevent mold and just general deterioration. If you eliminate all the stuff steam deposits on the walls, these rooms are much easier to clean.

As a rule, the bathroom and kitchen are repainted as often as presidents are elected. That means that paint build-up makes future painting tougher.

THANK YOU, MR. EDISON

Modern wiring is a marvel. Not that long ago there were still parts of the United States that weren't electrified. Now, especially with modern electrical codes, we've got power everywhere in the house and plenty of it. Power supplied by a utility company enters the house via a service connection. The amount of power coming in through those cables is much too strong to run any single item in the house (hook it up to your blender and you'd become part of your margarita), so it enters into a service panel. In new homes, this panel has circuit breakers; in older homes, fuses.

A COMPLETE WASTE OF TIME

The 3 Worst Things to Do About Ventilation

1. Keep windows painted shut.

2. Neglect to repair a broken fan.

3. Install a cheap fan.

The panel simply breaks up and distributes the power through your home in usable amounts. More goes to the kitchen and laundry than will go to a light switch. If you attempt to draw too much power out of a circuit, the fuse will burn out or the circuit breaker will trip and the flow of electricity stops. This prevents electrical mishaps and possible fires—sort of a system of governmental checks and balances for your house, without all the Congressional grandstanding.

Normally, most electrical problems occur when something is receiving current. It could be something simple like a light that's on, or when you've plugged the toaster oven and espresso maker into the same 60-year-old bedroom outlet because you decided to make breakfast in bed. Old wiring can fray and deteriorate. Over the years, various do-it-yourselfers, as well as contractors, tend to tap into wires and add on extra outlets or lights. This can be a really bad idea if the circuit they tie into cannot safely accommodate the extra demand for power.

WATERWORLD

Plumbing and wiring have some similarities. Water enters your home via a service line, a pipe running from the supplier's water main under the street. Once inside your house, the water is distributed to faucets and toilets through pipes of smaller diameter in order to control the pressure (even though a bathroom shower head connected directly to the service line would be awesome).

The water supply works under pressure. The smaller your service line, the less water, and thus water pressure, in your home, providing generations of battling siblings the revenge mechanism of flushing the toilet when a sib is in the shower. Newer homes have pretty much eliminated this problem.

Older plumbing often utilized galvanized steel pipes with lead soldered joints. Old drain lines can simply get clogged with decades of kitchen debris and grease if they aren't maintained and cleaned.

The normal problems you'll run into with any plumbing system include:

- Clogged drain lines
- Dripping faucets
- Leaks
- Poor pressure

BLOWING HOT AND COLD

Modern climate control has allowed us to populate parts of the country where no sane human being should be living, like Arizona when it's 120 degrees. Play your cards right and you can step from an air-conditioned house to an air-conditioned car and park at an air-conditioned office building.

Furnaces and boilers come in three main flavors: oil, gas, and electric. They generate heat and then distribute it through your house by:

- Blowing hot air through a system of sheetmetal ducts.
- Forcing hot water from boilers through pipes to radiators.

YOU'LL THANK YOURSELF LATER

Give your air conditioner and furnace a break. Plant shade trees in your yard to cut down on direct sunlight during the summer. In the winter months, more sun will be allowed in after the leaves have fallen, giving you some welcome light and warmth.

Moving steam from a boiler through pipes to radiators.

Ducts can be adjusted for greater or lesser heat flow depending on your preferences for a particular room. Furnaces today are far more efficient than the huge "octopus" types from the good old days.

Hot water and steam systems are very efficient as a rule and the heat they distribute is quite even and comfortable.

Air conditioning is distributed through ducts as well. When you have both heating and air conditioning systems, they use the same duct work.

UP, UP ON THE ROOF

Residential roofing materials include composition shingles, tile, cedar shakes, concrete, metal, and slate. Many older homes started out with shakes, which eventually get covered over with composition shingles during re-roofings. A properly installed and vented roof should last for years.

Most residential roofs these days are composition—asphalt-impregnated felt shingles coated with a layer of ceramic granules. Fiberglass shingles are also available, but are costly. Composition shingles are far cheaper than shakes, tile, or slate, and require almost no maintenance. Shake roofs are a complete nuisance to maintain and are not exactly fire retardant (wood + fire = more fire), though newer generation fireproof imitation shakes are available, but expensive.

SPUTTERING GUTTERS

All the water that lands on your roof has to go some-where, preferably somewhere away from your house. That's where gutters and downspouts come in. Gutters collect the water and downspouts carry it away.

Back in the olden days, gutters were made from wood, and sometimes copper (on expensive homes). If the idea of a wood gutter collecting water strikes you as strange, you're not alone. Wood gutters are attractive and expensive and a fine match for shake roofs. If you want something more practical, stick with continuous aluminum, by far the most common gutter system installed today.

When examining your gutters, you should look for:

- Leaks
- Excessive debris build-up
- Loose or hanging gutter sections
- Holes or other damage

FRAMES AND PANES

At one time, residential windows were made only of wood. Over the years, metal, aluminum, and vinyl windows have become available. Many new homes use vinyl, which is low maintenance and comparatively inexpensive. Older wood windows are single pane, that is, they have only one pane of glass. Code now usually requires insulated glass (two panes, or sometimes three, sandwiched together with an air space between them) to be installed in new homes.

IF YOU'RE SO
INCLINED

Old wooden windows are beautiful, but require a lot of maintenance. If you don't have time to spare, consider replacing them with metal, aluminum, or vinyl.

New windows need little maintenance. The jury is still out regarding the longevity of vinyl windows, but with careful use they should last indefinitely. Older wood windows should last indefinitely, too, but they require more vigilant maintenance. Many people in older homes prefer the look of original wood windows, but are often at a loss as to how to repair and maintain them.

You should check your windows for:

■ Leaks and condensation

■ Ease (or difficulty) of movement

■ Broken glass or hardware

■ Deteriorated paint or putty (wood windows)

Pretty as a Picture

Paint follows the same code as the police: it protects and serves. In a world full of water and moisture, paint and its colleagues, like polyurethane and varnishes, repel water and protect our houses. Paint also serves by allowing us to express our artistic side with color.

Prior to the 1950s, there were few choices in residential paints. Oil was king, and it gushed onto walls and woodwork alike. Oil-based paint is slowly being phased out and will not be seen much in the future except for special applications. The new king is latex, a water-based product that is superior to oil in many respects.

If you have a new home, unless some weird custom finish was specified, all the walls will be done in latex. The woodwork will be done in either latex enamel or some exotic, fast-drying material that has to be sprayed on and is just about impossible to touch up with a brush. Painters use this because its drying time is so short they can spray multiple coats in one day, and finish their work faster.

Older homes, especially those built before the 1950s, will contain a combination of latex and oil-based paints. Often, the woodwork, which started out with oil-based paint, will have been recoated with latex at some later time.

If your woodwork has only oil-based paint on it, you will have to prepare it properly before you paint with latex. There is also the issue of lead-based paint that you must be aware of if your older home needs extensive stripping or scraping prior to painting. For more information, see Chapter 14.

NOT QUITE EDEN

Yards serve several purposes. They act as buffers between neighbors, maintaining enough psychic distance to keep us all civilized. A lawn gives kids someplace safe to play and dogs somewhere to roam. For gardening types, a yard can provide a horticultural palette or even an urban farm. If your only interest is in maintaining a buffer zone, hire a lawn service. I am a big advocate of hiring someone to cut the lawn.

YOU'LL THANK YOURSELF LATER

Be certain anyone you hire to work on your house or mow your lawn is licensed and bonded. If an unlicensed Mr. or Ms. Handyguy falls off a ladder while cleaning your gutters, you can be liable, since you can be considered an employer who did the hiring.

Getting Sense on Your Side

The Crazy Way	The Lazy Way
Fertilize, water, mow, and dispose of grass clippings from a traditional lawn: Just what I wanted for my birthday, a 6-pack of lawnmower blades	Use ground cover and boulders in your yard: What's a lawnmower?
Neglect regular roof maintenance: Well, if the moss builds up a bit more, it should stop the drips in our bedroom	Clean roof regularly and check for leaks: how dry we are!
Ignore furnace maintenance: If technology is worth a damn, the furnace will replace itself	Have yearly check-ups and regular filter replacement: a call to the furnace company and 4 new filters— warm as a toaster!
Look for a wall stud by knocking on the wall and guessing: Maybe I can glue this picture on the wall and cover up all my test holes at the same time	Use an electric stud finder: "X" marks the spot

Put a Lid on It: A Roof Overhead

You inspected your roof at the beginning of the summer when the world was warm and happy. You found a couple of suspect areas, but there wasn't a cloud in sight. Doing your best Scarlett O'Hara you figured there's always tomorrow. Uh oh, tomorrow arrived, windy and rainy, and leaking right over your bed. It's hard to sleep, let alone be romantic, when you're tuned to the rhythm of a bucket filling up, one drip at a time.

Even the best roofs need some looking after. A shingle can blow loose or some flashing (the sheetmetal used to waterproof certain sections of a roof) may need to be sealed. But with a little maintenance, your roof will keep you dry and the buckets in the garage where they belong.

CHECK IT OUT

Roofs come in all different shapes and sizes, including extreme peaks, which are found mostly in older houses. They look very cool until it comes time to replace or repair them. As the slope goes up, so does the price.

New roof or old, have it looked at at least once a year, or after any major windstorm. You should be on the lookout for:

- Missing or loose shingles
- Leaks
- Moss build-up
- Aging shingles
- Sags

If you have an exposed attic space, an inside inspection is painless! Pick a sunny day and take a:

- Flashlight or emergency light
- Pocket knife
- Pen and paper
- Bucket
- Thin wire

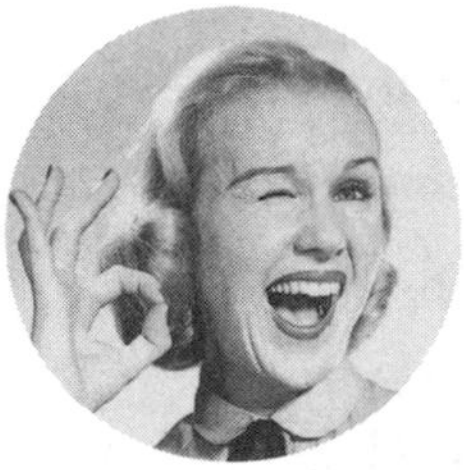

You'll need the flashlight or emergency light since few attic crawl spaces have lighting. Carefully make your may around, especially if your attic doesn't have a plywood floor covering the joists! One wrong move and you can stick a foot through the ceiling below—standard fare in TV sitcoms when Dad decides to check for leaks. Take

QUICK n' PAINLESS

Hate climbing ladders? If you can get a good view of your roof from the street or a neighbor's house, use a pair of binoculars for your inspection. Especially if it's a newer roof, this will give you a pretty good idea of its condition.

one or two small pieces of plywood with you to stand on, and move them around as you make your way through the attic. Snowshoes can also do the trick.

Check for any areas, especially near the chimney, where daylight might be coming through the roof. This is very unlikely with a new roof. If you do see daylight, shove a piece of thin wire up and through the hole or gap so you can find it later out on the roof.

Check for water stains and probe any suspicious areas with the knife blade. If they're soft—and certainly if they're wet—mark the location on your paper. Use it as a rough map of your roof so you'll have an idea of where to look for holes and gaps from the outside, or have it done by a roofer. Place a bucket under the suspect area just in case it drips again.

A Word or Two About Leaks

Leaks can be notoriously difficult to find and repair, even for seasoned roofers. Water can enter at a high point on a roof, but not show up until it flows down a rafter and decides it wants to get off. So a wet spot may or may not be directly under a leak.

Roof leaks usually don't go right through a shingle. That's too easy. They leak at the:

- Flashing
- Chimney
- Skylights
- Vents
- Valleys

IF YOU'RE SO
INCLINED

It's fruitful to do an inspection on extremely rainy days, too! If you do have any leaks, that's when they'll show up.

QUICK n PAINLESS

If you're a little uncom-
fortable on ladders, you
don't have to carry everything up to the roof as you
climb. Put it in a bucket,
tie a rope to it, climb up
with the other end of the
rope, and haul it up.

The chimney, skylights, and roof vents all require that holes be cut through the roof. Obviously, this is where a roof can leak! Valleys form where two slopes of a roof meet (they look like troughs). They are covered in strategic areas with sheetmetal called flashing.

Have a Leak?

Check out the Most Likely Sources First. You'll Need :

- Ladder
- Shoes with rubber soles
- Patching compound
- Putty knife
- Hammer and nail
- Rope or bailing wire
- Automotive undercoating

1 Go to your local lumber yard or home improvement center. Ask the sales clerk for an appropriate roof sealant for the repairs you need to do. If it comes in a tube, buy two of them. You'll also need a caulking gun. Buy a quart if the sealant comes by the can.

2 Carefully climb up onto the roof. If you're headed to the second floor, hammer a nail into the house and tie the ladder to it with some rope or bailing wire. Otherwise, if the ladder slips or blows away, you can be stuck!

3 Check the area, or suspected area, of the leak. Look for loose roofing nails, damaged shingles, and any flashing. This is one time when more is better, so coat any suspicious area with your patching material. Smear it in completely with your putty knife, a simple job. If your metal flashing

looks suspect, spray it with automotive undercoating. This is a quick and effective metal repair.

4 Look at your valleys. You may have a roof so old that metal flashing wasn't used as it is today—just shingles! If you see any cracks, smear away.

Roofing Materials

Over time, and depending on the location, a variety of materials have been used for roofs. In parts of Great Britain, thatch, which is basically straw, is still used in some situations. These days, here in the former colonies, roofing materials are less combustible. They include:

- Wood shakes
- Composition shingles
- Metal
- Tile
- Concrete shingles and shakes

Up on Top with the Shakes

Years ago, most roofs were made from cedar shakes or shingles. Sometimes, redwood was also used. If you have an attic with an exposed ceiling, you'll probably see this first layer of roofing nailed onto narrow strips of wood called skip sheathing.

Builders continue to use cedar shakes today when they install cedar roofs. With a lower pitch and inferior materials, new cedar roofs aren't all that long lasting and maintenance is a nuisance.

QUICK ⬤ PAINLESS

If you have an elusive leak, put a bucket or other container under it to catch the water. Place a weighted tarp over the area of the roof you think is the source of the leak and check during the next rainstorm to see if you were right.

If you're buying a new home under construction or replacing a cedar shake roof, don't install a wood roof! If you really like the looks of a cedar roof, consider alternatives like concrete or aluminum shingles with a similar appearance.

Maintenance on cedar shake roofs includes:

1. Regular removal of debris.

2. Replacement of missing or worn shingles.

3. Re-coating with preservative sealer.

4. Coating with fire retardant.

Avoid the Shakes, Hire a Roofer

Cedar shake roofs are not homeowner friendly when it comes to maintenance. Before you go snooping for a conspiracy among the wood shakes manufacturers of America, remember that a lot of people like the look of shake roofs and that's why builders install them. I don't recommend you get up on yours to inspect it, though. Hire a roofer or licensed contractor who cleans and seals shake roofs. It's not inexpensive, but it's very easy to do.

1. Use recommendations from friends, neighbors, and real estate agents.

2. Check for a license and a bond.

3. Ask to look at recent similar work and talk to these customers.

4. Agree to a price before any work begins.

5. Get at least two bids.

The ideal climate for a cedar roof doesn't exist, at least not in this universe. It would be dry, overcast, windless, and without insects of any kind. The roof would be located 10 miles from the closest tree so no leaves or needles would ever touch it. Birds would respect a

1,000-foot no-fly zone around it. And the shakes would have been cut from a hitherto unknown grove of ancient cedar giants, growing up tall and true and genetically perfect. Finally, the trees would be fed and massaged in the manner of Japanese cows who later become kobi steak dinners.

Keeping It Pretty and Yourself Dry

New shake roofs, properly installed and vented, can last for years if they're maintained. If it's new, you're off to a good start!

Maintenance varies depending on where you live. In the damp Northwest, where a lot of people really seem to like living in the shadows of fir and cedar trees, you may have to clean needles off a shake roof twice a year or more. If it's constantly in the shade and has a hard time drying out for long periods of time, you may need to apply sealer every year.

If you want to do some of your own maintenance on a new cedar roof, you'll need:

- Corkers
- Ladder
- Leaf blower
- Moss cleaner
- Garden hose

No, corkers are not what your parents use to call really fun parties. Well, maybe they did. For your purposes, they're special strap-on spiked shoes that keep you from damaging the shakes (and from falling off the

QUICK n' PAINLESS

As far as maintenance goes, the next time you're watering the flowers, give the roof a rinse to keep any dirt off it. Pat yourself on the back for being such a clever homeowner!

roof). Some rental shops have them if you don't want to buy them.

A leaf blower will clear the majority of needles and leaves from your roof without damaging the shakes. If you happen to blow a shake loose from the roof, it's better to find out now than during a wind storm!

If you don't have a blower, a garden hose will do the trick, but it may take longer. Shoot the water down onto the shingles from the top of the roof so you don't get any water underneath them. If you have moss or mildew problems, apply moss cleaner according to directions. Check your gutters for debris after you've cleaned the roof!

You may not be at all comfortable running around on your roof. Many people are not. In this case, the laziest way may be the best way—hire the work out. Sleep well knowing the roof over your head is in good hands.

Shake Surgery

Sadly, for cedar trees chopped down in the prime of their lives to become roofs in a Seattle suburb, many shake roofs are ill-maintained. Due to neglect, some barely last 10 years before they turn into compost, harboring moss and small plants.

If your roof is in such condition, have it evaluated by two competent roofers. If it's time to replace it, strongly consider a composition roof made from asphalt shingles. Roofers usually work very quickly—they have to because they're exposing the house to the weather. Go to work, let them do their job, and come home to a new, high-quality roof!

IF YOU'RE SO
INCLINED

As long as you're hosing the roof, water the garden below at the same time.

Compose Yourself with Composition Shingles

Composition shingles are the most common roofing material used on new homes. They are long-lasting and easy to install. Most are combinations of either asphalt, impregnated felt coated with colored stone, or fiberglass products. Best of all, they require almost no maintenance! This is truly a lazy roofing material!

Armchair Repair with Composition Roofs

New roof? Relax! Basically you have nothing to do except give it the eye once a year or so and forget about it. If you have any moss or mildew build-up, spray it with a moss killer made for composition roofs and follow directions. That's it, it's as easy as it gets. Unless you get leaks inside the house, you're home free.

One warning: Never use a pressure washer on a composition roof. The high pressure will force water under the shingles and wash away too many of the ceramic granules embedded in them!

Same as for new roofs, unless you have leaks. If you don't have leaks or moss, all you need to do is monitor the condition of the shingles. Look for:

- Curled edges
- Loss of ceramic granules
- Brittle shingles

You want a roof to live out its maximum life span before replacing it, but, like giving birth, it's pretty tough to time it perfectly. Get an opinion from a trusted roofing

A COMPLETE WASTE OF TIME

The 3 Worst Things to Do with an Old Shake Roof That Needs Replacing

1. Meticulously repair broken shakes.

2. Professionally clean and seal the roof.

3. Keep it until it really leaks.

contractor. If it has to go, get a couple of bids and have a roofer do the job.

If You Need a New Roof

Old houses almost always have multiple roofs (one installed over another). Three layers of roofing is pretty much the maximum a house can hold, unless you want your rafters to bow in like a house in a cartoon show.

If you already have three layers of roofing, you will need a tear-off done. This work includes:

1. Removing all the old layers of roofing.

2. Installing new plywood or similar sheathing over the rafters.

3. Installing new roofing.

4. Hauling off and disposing of all debris.

It's a ton of work and roofers often work late into the day to get as much finished as possible. In very hot climates, they start at the first morning light—which doesn't exactly make friends with any of the neighbors— and stop when the heat gets too intense.

There is a natural order to life. Roofers are part of it. Don't fight it, do the work you do best, relax and have a roofing company replace your roof.

Make My Day with Metal

Metal roofs are slowly coming into use in new residential construction. The advantages are obvious: They are fire-proof, durable, and easy to maintain and install.

If you suspect leaks, call a roofer to come and recaulk your roof.

Smile with Tile

Tile roofs have traditionally been installed in certain styles of homes, such as Tudors and Spanish-influenced designs. They are heavy, and require beefed-up framing to support them. They also last for years and years.

Tile is a mixed blessing. It's got longevity, but it's not maintenance friendly for a do-it-your-self homeowner.

Stay off it and call a roofer who handles tile to inspect it every few years, especially if you suspect any leaks. It's money well spent.

Concrete Shingles

These are in the same category as tile. If you have a leak, leave it to an experienced roofer. And if you don't, enjoy the extra free time having a low-maintenance roof gives you.

Goofs on roofs

Replacing a roof should be fast work. Have you ever watched an inexperienced homeowner do it, working part time or using a few vacation days? One sudden storm with a roof torn off and all of Grandma's treasures in the attic are ruined. Spend your vacation days on vacation, not on your roof!

Congratulations! You understand reasonable limitations and when to call in outside help. Some people never learn this. Take yourself out to dinner at your favorite restaurant with company you enjoy.

The Lazy Way

Getting Sense on Your Side

The Crazy Way	The Lazy Way
Let moss build up on your roof	Do periodic cleanings
Replace your old shake with a new shake roof roof	Replace it with a composition roof
Never inspect for leaks	Do regular inspections
Replace your roof yourself	Hire a roofing contractor
Ignore a shake roof	Clean and seal it regularly
Inspect your tile roof for leaks	Hire an experienced contractor

Chapter eight

Gutters: Down and Out

If you live in certain parts of the Southwest, you can skip this section. You don't have any gutters! Your gutter maintenance is the easiest yet—none. There's plenty of room down there for all you gutterphobic types if you want to steer clear, but then you'll have to get used to snakes and droughts and . . .

For the rest of us, gutters are a good thing to have on our houses, even if the only time we notice them is when they're overflowing or demanding to be cleaned. Take care of your gutters and they'll take care of you.

Living High and Dry

Gutters and downspouts (the vertical sections of pipe that attach to a gutter to drain water away from a house) are designed with one purpose in mind: to collect water running off your roof and direct it away from the house. This is a great theory if:

The best preventive maintenance for gutters is keeping them clean. A simple scooping and rinsing twice a year, in most areas, will keep them from collecting water and overflowing. Excessive water can turn into ice problems in the winter.

1. Your gutters are sloped correctly to allow water to flow toward the downspouts.

2. Your gutter hangers (these attach the gutters to the house) are intact.

3. You don't have any broken seams.

Water Doesn't Flow Uphill

Properly installed gutters will slope ever so slightly toward the downspouts. If they aren't sloped properly, water and debris will collect in them and the gutters can pull away from the roof! Poorly designed or maintained gutter systems are one of the major causes of water and moisture problems in basements and crawl spaces!

If this is a problem, call a gutter contractor to re-slope your gutters. If it ends up being a bigger problem than you thought, you may need a new section of gutter installed. Avoid the hassle and contract it out!

Gutter hangers can come loose for two main reasons:

1. They weren't properly installed in the first place.

2. The gutter isn't sloping correctly and is collecting water and pulling away from the roof.

To reattach a hanger, first hold the gutter up to its old position and have someone fill it with water. If the water doesn't run out, you need to change the position of the hanger. If you find that it won't fit, call a gutter contractor, but not the same one who did the original installation!

Seams occur in gutters wherever two pieces of gutter are joined. With new continuous aluminum gutters, the usual choice in new housing, the seams appear at the corners and near the downspouts. If these are leaking (easy enough to tell in the rain), go to your favorite home improvement center or hardware store and:

1. Buy the appropriate caulk and caulk gun, if needed.

2. Caulk the gutter on a dry day.

3. Test with a hose after the caulking has cured.

Totally Awesome Aluminum

The very best new gutters are continuous, or seamless, aluminum. Each section is extruded and cut to length in single pieces to fit your house on every side. The installer shows up with a roll of aluminum and an extruding machine. Flat metal goes in one end, a gutter comes out the other. It doesn't get any easier than this! And it's the best thing for your house, too. Aluminum gutters hold much more water than traditional wood gutters, and they never rot!

If it's time to replace your original wood gutters, and you're not a historical purist, do it with aluminum!

The Real Scoop

Downspouts drain into one of three places:

- A storm drain
- A French drain
- A splash block

A storm drain collects storm runoff from streets and outside house drains. This is the best hook-up for gutters

QUICK ɪɴ PAINLESS

You can always check the flow and drainage of your gutters by filling them up with a hose one length at a time. Do it on a dry day; it's easier than trying to find the problem during a rainstorm.

and downspouts and is most common on new houses built near storm drain systems.

Some homes use French drains, which are pits or trenches filled with some type of crushed stone. They are dug far enough away from a house to prevent any water from backing up into the basement or crawl space. They're covered with soil so you'll never know they're in your yard. I'm not sure how the French feel about having a drain named after them. Personally, I find French fries far more appealing.

Splash blocks are flipper-shaped (the diving gear, not the dolphin) plastic or concrete pads placed at the end of a downspout to channel water away from the house. Many people ignore them, even turn them the wrong way so water slopes toward the house. Simple splash block maintenance consists of:

1. Keeping dirt and debris out of the block.

2. Making sure it's slanted away from the house.

Downspouts only work if the gutters are clear and can carry water to them. All gutters need the same basic maintenance:

1. Scoop out all debris.

2. Rinse out dirt and small remaining debris with a hose.

Do you have more gutters than you can clean in one shot? No problem. You can:

1. Break your cleaning down into small sections.

2. Spend no more than 20 minutes at a time cleaning.

3. Clean before the rains come and the weather is still warm!

There's no way around scooping, but there's a way to speed it up and quicken the task. Use a Gutter Getter, a plastic, flexible scoop that cleans new aluminum gutters faster than small garden shovels. Call Working Products, 800-569-7326, for ordering information. (Note: The Gutter Getter doesn't fit some types of older gutters.

To scoop out your gutters, you'll need:

- Latex gloves
- Ladder
- Scooping tool
- Bucket
- Garden hose

In addition to nature's debris, gutters can collect ceramic granules that wash off your shingles along with any adhesive residue they might carry. You can develop a rash if you handle this material with your bare hands, so be sure to wear gloves.

Ladders can dent aluminum gutters if they are not laid against them carefully! It's easier to use a step ladder for all lower gutters.

QUICK ⬤ PAINLESS

If the leaves in your gutters are dry, and you're raking the yard anyway, you can use a leaf blower to get them out, and rake up the debris with the other leaves.

Gutters have a tendency to collect leaves, pine needles, acorns, and whatever small toys your kids manage to toss into them. Shovel everything into a bucket so you don't have to clean it up again by sweeping or raking it out of your yard. Empty the bucket into your trash container, rinse the gutters, and your job is done!

Cleaning gutters is a nuisance, but a very lazy choice given the alternative: moisture damage from the overflow! Water cascading over the sides of gutters and onto a house is a guaranteed future paint or rot problem—a lot more work than a gutter cleaning once or twice a year.

Well, There Were All These Trees. . .

For years and years, the common residential gutter system consisted of cedar, or sometimes redwood, gutters and galvanized metal downspouts. Casual observation would dictate that a wood gutter wouldn't seem the wisest choice to contain water and be subjected to all kinds of temperature extremes. Maybe some early cedar gutter association had some really awesome lobbyists influencing national building codes.

Wood gutters are very handsome and fitting on older homes. That's where their charm comes to a crashing halt. A wood gutter is more subject to leaks from:

- Rot
- Worn downspout holes
- Cracked seams

In addition to normal scooping and cleaning, wood gutters need to be treated with a preservative or sealer, just like those marvelous shake roofs. Wood gutters can be treated with:

- Linseed oil
- Tar-type products
- Liquid epoxy or fiberglass

Linseed oil is the traditional preservative for wood gutters. A time long ago, Dad or the neighborhood handy guy would come around and clean the gutters, allow them to dry completely, and then pour in linseed oil. The oil would prevent the wood from cracking, and seal out water. An easy task, a no brainer. Somewhere along the line, like maybe 40 years ago, the linseed oil started collecting dust in the garage, and the gutters began to rot out.

Today, some homes still have these original gutters, only now they're slightly rot-and-leak-challenged. Linseed oil will help only if your gutters are intact. If yours are, oiling them is almost pleasant. You'll need:

- Linseed oil
- Squeeze bottle
- Old paint brush

Clean the gutters and allow them to dry completely. Pour the linseed oil (you can buy it at a paint store) into your squeeze bottle. Liberally squirt the oil into the gutters and spread with the paint brush. You're done!

QUICK ᴨ PAINLESS

Linseed oil needs to be stored in an airtight container. A partially empty can will have enough air inside it to affect the oil, so pour it into a smaller container to help preserve it.

It's especially important to keep wooden gutters clear of debris so they can drain and dry out. The longer they remain wet, the faster they deteriorate. Standing water and wood is a bad combination—keep them clean!

Rough Flowing

If Dad or the local handy guy hasn't been around to oil the gutters for a few decades, you'll probably have bigger problems like cracks and holes. Specific products for coating gutters are available at lumber stores and home improvement centers. They are very similar to roofing tar.

These products are applied to a clean, dry wood gutter with a small putty knife. They are spread like cake icing (well, not quite as artistically) on the bottom of the gutter. Eventually, however, they dry out and shrink at the edges and then they tend to trap water underneath them, compounding your problems. I don't recommend using them at all.

Liquid epoxy and liquid fiberglass are tougher than the tar products and soak into the wood rather than just coating the surface. As in oiling, you pour the mixed material into the gutter and spread it with an old paint brush. If you have a lot of area to cover, you'll need to buy a lot of epoxy or fiberglass material. Read the instructions on the can! These materials dry fast, so work quickly and don't mix more than you can use within a 10-minute period or so.

If your gutters are ready to go on to gutter heaven, what's the easiest way out? Call a couple of gutter contractors and get some bids. You should consider replacing your wood gutters when:

1. They leak excessively in many locations.

2. It's apparent that they're too small to handle the water runoff from your roof.

3. Whole sections or pieces are missing.

   If you're a purist, you can get new wood gutters, but be prepared to pay the price! They are several times more expensive than aluminum gutters and still carry less water. If you want hassle-free gutters, go with aluminum. All you'll ever do is clean them, and you can forget about the linseed oil!

Prohibitive Plastic

Plastic gutters are the do-it-your-selfer alternative to continuous aluminum gutters. Installing these is not a lazy approach! You would have to:

1. Remove and dispose of all existing gutters and downspouts.

2. Measure and purchase plastic gutters.

3. Install the gutters at the proper slope.

4. Make trips back to the store for all the extra connectors, elbows, and odd pieces you didn't count on needing.

   The cost of plastic gutter systems, specifically all the fittings, can really add up. If you need new gutters, do yourself a favor: call a gutter contractor to install aluminum gutters. Then all you'll have to do is clean them a couple of times a year. That's the easy part of the job!

IF YOU'RE SO
INCLINED

If you do install new wood gutters, for historic or aesthetic reasons, be sure to coat them with linseed oil before they're attached to the house! It's hands down easier to do it this way than from a ladder!

Getting Time on Your Side

	The Old Way	**The Lazy Way**
Install plastic gutters yourself	Spend lots of time and money	A contractor with a fair price—Spend no time at all
Give your gutters regular annual cleanings vs. leaving their fragile ecosystems alone	Water, water everywhere to slosh through	Clean them so fast you might go into business
Repair and repaint deteriorated wood gutters vs. installing aluminum ones	Be sentimental and have to replace them anyway	Go Gutter King and spend no time at all
Use linseed oil on your wooden gutters vs. ignoring them	Replace them when they rot	Spend no time brushing on the oil
Check to be sure your downspouts are draining away from the house vs. ignoring them	Water your basement to keep it from drying out	Go splashblocks

Strain-Free Siding Maintenance

Wood siding does for the walls of your house what roofing shingles do for the top: it keeps the weather out and keeps you cozy inside. Wood has been a traditional siding choice since the Mayflower days for one good reason—trees were abundant and cheap. But it's not as though there was a big U-Cut-It tree farm run by some guy in a plaid shirt and funny orange cap who billed colonists for every tree cut. All you needed was an ax, and that oak tree that had been standing since time immemorial was yours for the taking.

SIDING SENTIMENT

These days, we have more choices. In addition to wood, builders use brick, stucco, vinyl, synthetic wood siding, and concrete products on the exteriors of houses. Before vinyl showed up, aluminum siding was the hot product for re-siding. But it isn't as cost effective today. The type of siding you have will, to some extent, be determined by the age of your house and any remodeling done to it over the years.

Siding has an eternal quality to it: Keep it painted and sealed and, theoretically, it will last indefinitely. Attend to it and you won't have to replace it—fires, termites, and runaway cars notwithstanding.

"Mythical" Siding

"Mythical" because today it costs a small fortune, this siding came from old-growth cedar trees. It was very straight-grained (this is good) and had few, if any, knots (this is also good). The same trees were a source for shingles. Today, siding made from this wood would exceed what an entire house cost when its mythical siding was installed.

One of the biggest problems with old siding is failing paint—an entire category in itself.

Lead Me to the Lead

It's safe to assume that at least some parts of most old houses were painted with lead-based paint. This is considered by the Environmental Protection Agency (EPA) and other government agencies to be evil incarnate and must be dealt with accordingly. Lead-based paint was banned in 1978. Theoretically, if your home was painted before then, especially during the 1960s or earlier, lead-based paint could have been used. Legally, there are very specific procedures you must follow when dealing with the removal of lead-based paint. If your siding has peeling and blistering paint that must be scraped and sanded prior to painting, you should remember what Mr. Rogers advised: "Like yourself" (and don't touch the paint).

The easiest way to deal with deteriorated lead-based paint (after you've had it tested to determine if it really contains lead) would be to cover it up with new siding. Lead abatement, or removal, is very expensive. Your local government may mandate that lead abatement be done only by a qualified contractor, or make your life difficult if you try to do it yourself. If your contractor doesn't follow the rules, you could all be in legal hot water if the neighbors take you to court for poisoning them and all of their future offspring. Another option is to remove and replace the siding, which will involve some abatement costs, but they'll be nowhere near the cost of stripping off the old paint.

The easy way out isn't cheap, but it will resolve the problem.

If your paint is in good shape, follow the simple path: leave the lead alone and repaint as needed.

Rembrandt Unleashed

Even the best paint jobs on old homes develop occasional blisters or bubbles. Sometimes they're hollow and sometimes they're full of water! Do a speedy repair and no one will ever know you touched it. To repair blisters and bubbles you'll need:

- Putty knife
- Exterior Spackle
- 100-grit sandpaper
- Foam paint brushes
- Fast-dry primer
- Paint

Pop the bubble and lightly scrape back the paint with your putty knife. Carefully dispose of all paint chips. Use

IF YOU'RE SO
INCLINED

The EPA and the National Lead Information Center have free booklets and information regarding lead-based paint. These are listed in our "More Lazy Stuff" section at the end of the book.

the same knife to fill the space, up to and over the edges of the intact paint, with a thin coat of Spackle. Go and have a cup of coffee while the Spackle dries.

Sand the Spackle and prime it. Fast-drying primer really speeds up the job! When the primer has dried, paint the entire board or shingle, not just the Spackled area. You don't want anyone to know you patched it, do you? It's less likely to show if the whole board is the same color. A quick job and you'll look like a pro!

If you used an oil-based primer, toss the brush out. If you used latex-based primer or paint, you can clean the brush or toss it. Although some painters will argue the point, either primer will work with latex pain. Foam brushes, usable with either type of paint, are cheap and easily replaceable.

Faking It

Repainting old houses can be a lot of work. They usually have more detail than new homes and more preparation work to do. And there's all that lead-based paint!

If your paint is in good shape, and you like the color, give it a lather and a rinse and forget about it. You'll need a few things, such as:

- Garden hose
- House/car washer
- Soap

Home centers and some hardware stores sell house/car washer systems for cleaning windows, siding, and automobiles. They consist of a set of aluminum or

plastic pipes that screw together. Look for a system that will give you a total of around 15 feet in length, and attach sections as needed. You can control the distribution of soap from a container that attaches to the hose end. The end section that does the scrubbing takes a brush attachment.

This is as simple as it gets! No pressure washers, no compressors, no expensive equipment. Just an easy-to-store, easy-to-use tool that fits neatly on a shelf in the garage or basement. It's perfect for washing pollution, dirt, and auto exhaust off your house and keeping your paint looking like new.

Crack Attacks

The main structural problems you will run into with wood siding are:

- Loosening, cracking, or weathering
- Opening joints
- Warped or missing shingles

Wood likes to move and groove as it gets exposed to moisture and different temperatures. When wood is kiln dried (a kiln is a kind of oven for the lumber crowd) it has a low moisture content and is more or less stable for most uses. If it gets exposed to moisture in the form of rain and snow, it soaks it up and expands. When the weather warms up, it shrinks again. If it does this rumba one too many times, it begins to split along its grain and get rough and splintery.

Just wash one side of your house at a time. Give yourself half an hour to do the job, and then put everything away. Spread the work out over several days or two weekends, and relax.

The Lazy Way

Usually, siding loosens because a nail gives way and needs to be replaced, and splits can occur along the grain of the wood near a nail. They're all easy to patch up, but do your repairs on a warm, dry day. You'll need a few items, including:

- Ladder
- Hammer and shingle nails
- Paint scraper
- Exterior Spackle
- Sandpaper
- Exterior caulking and caulk gun
- Putty knife
- Wet rag
- Primer and paint
- Exterior glue

Siding tends to come loose at the corners of a house where—a beautiful finishing touch in old homes—the boards are mitered together. Over time, the joints can separate.

Solution? It's as easy as 1,2,3:

1 Nail the siding back in place with galvanized siding nails.

2 Caulk the seam with exterior latex caulking.

3 Paint the caulking and the head of the nail.

Think of how much stripping, sanding, and paint feathering you won't have to do if you Spackle and fill. Use the time you save to watch others do all the work on "This Old House."

Cracked siding can be even simpler to fix, even if the crack is deep. If it's an old crack and the siding isn't loose, you'll need to:

1. Fill the crack with caulking (if the crack is deep, fill it half way, allow the caulking to dry, and fill it again).

2. Smooth the caulking with a putty knife so that it's flush with the siding.

3. Paint the entire board when the caulking is dry.

A more thorough repair would include epoxy filler, sanding, more filler, priming, and painting. But caulking works quite well and is a lot faster!

If the siding is loose along the crack or split:

1. Pry the siding out slightly along its bottom edge.

2. Squeeze some exterior-grade glue along the split.

3. Nail both parts of the siding to the wall.

4. Wipe off any excess glue with a wet rag.

Weathered siding may look like a chore to repair, but it doesn't have to be. If you have a lot of it, like the entire side of your house, you might consider replacing it and starting fresh. If only a few minor areas have weathered, all you'll have to do is:

1. Scrape away any loose paint, remembering to pay attention to lead-based paint regulations.

QUICK ⚙ PAINLESS

If you're inexperienced with a putty knife, wet it slightly before you do your final draw across the Spackle. This will help smooth the material and give you a more even finish.

2 Lightly sand any splintered wood.

3 Prime the wood (oil primer is often a better choice on weathered siding).

4 Skim over the wood with exterior Spackle, pressing it in and smoothing it with a putty knife so you have a thin coat of material.

5 After it's dried, sand the Spackle.

6 Prime the Spackle repairs.

7 Paint each entire board you repaired.

Spackle can be sanded the same day you apply it. While it's drying, put your feet up and read the Sunday paper. After you've painted, stand back and admire your work!

When the junctions, (called joints) where two pieces of siding meet, separate they need to be filled to keep water out. Siding is kind of a closed system: Open it up to the weather and it rebels by splitting, weathering, and cracking. When you come across any joints that have begun to split open, especially at the corners of your house, caulk and paint. A quick squirt of latex caulking, wipe, touch up with paint, and you're all done!

Mingle with Your Shingles

Cedar shingles, because they have three edges exposed to the weather, have a tendency to bow and warp on the weathered sides of a house (usually the southern side).

IF YOU'RE SO
INCLINED

If you must replace a piece of siding on an old house, buy a top grade of new material rather than one that's rough or has knots. It will more closely match the original, and you won't have to treat the knots before you paint.

Even the best paint jobs can't always prevent this. Sometimes a warped shingle can be nailed flat, but often it will simply crack when you attempt to nail it.

The easiest approach? Leave it alone! Shingles were installed in two layers so that, even if the top layer looks like it's having a bad hair day, your house will remain protected. Besides, on a weathered wall you'll usually have not one, but many warped and cupped shingles. You would almost have to replace all of them—a big expense just to get a prettier wall!

An occasional missing shingle is another matter. These should be replaced. You will need:

- Hammer and shingle nails
- New shingle
- Primer and paint

YOU'LL THANK YOURSELF LATER

Be sure to thoroughly prime and paint the bottom edge of each shingle. This is a very porous area which soaks up a lot of paint and water if it isn't well-sealed.

Shingles come in different grades. They also come in bundles, which contain more than you'll ever need for a couple of repairs! Unless you want a pile of shingles kicking around your garage, you might consider trying to buy a couple of them from an owner or contractor who is re-shingling a house in your neighborhood. Even used shingles from a house that's being torn down will work if you can find a few intact.

If you have to buy an entire bundle of shingles, tell the lumber yard clerk you need a finish shingle (#1 or #2). And there's always the chance they may have a couple of loose ones that fell out of a bundle—or maybe came out of a package they opened for a customer like you who only needed a few.

Before you install it, prime and paint the shingle. It's a lot easier when it's unattached! Tuck the shingle up into the wall, keeping the bottom edge level with the surrounding shingles. Two shingle nails and you're all done.

Living in a Plastic World

Vinyl siding is probably the material that's closest to essentially no maintenance. Hose it off once in a while, that's it. Its appearance and curb appeal to prospective buyers is another matter, but personal taste is just that, personal. Fine-grained, expensive cedar siding looks terrific, stained or painted. And it will look terrific every time you stain and paint it, over and over again.

Vinyl siding just needs to be washed. You spend most of your time inside your house. Unless you set up your easy chair outside and endlessly contemplate your siding as an art form, do you really care if it's vinyl or not? The longevity of vinyl siding has yet to be determined, but look at the alternative: paint (ladders, brushes, gallons of paint, rags, clean-up, caulking) or wash (garden hose). This is a decision?

More Unnaturals

There are various synthetic sidings available that give the appearance of wood, and hold paint very well, but they're produced in a factories, not forests, from wood leftovers. Their longevity is also unknown. One brand, the infamous premier version LP (Louisiana-Pacific) Inner Seal Siding, hasn't held up well at all judging by the multi-million dollar settlement the company is paying

QUICK n' PAINLESS

No matter what you do to it, an old house will never be a new house again. Don't worry about its limitations. Giving up the idea of perfection and enjoying your free time is easier than you think!

out to dissatisfied customers. Apparently some whiners complained about mushrooms growing out of their siding in damp climates. More to the point, the siding absorbs water, swells, and basically disintegrates. After going back to the drawing board, Louisiana-Pacific came out with the new, improved version. (If you think you may have the original LP Inner Seal Siding, call 800-245-2722 pronto for recall information.)

In theory, these types of siding products should last indefinitely. Hardiplank is a fiber-cement siding that gives the appearance of wood. What more could you ask? Well, the test of time, for one. In the interim, if you've got any synthetic wood siding products, all you have to do is give your house a bath once a year and paint it every 8 to 10 years or as needed. It's easy, but keep an eye out for any recall notices.

Hit the Bricks

Brick houses can be mostly ignored except for painting the trim, windows, and doors once in a while. This strategy works as long as the bricks stay intact. Think of bricks as a veneer or a siding on your house. They're just there to keep the weather out (well, that and to give brick masons jobs). For the most part, brick homes are built up and around standard wood framing. The bricks are attached to the framing with brick ties (usually), which are wires attached to the framing and set into the mortar.

The bricks themselves are held together with mortar, a cement-based mix that eventually deteriorates in cold,

A COMPLETE WASTE OF TIME

The 3 Worst Ways to Treat Synthetic Sidings

1. Ignore maintenance and cleaning.

2. Think you don't have to inspect them because they'll last forever.

3. Use them to cover rotted siding without finding the cause of the rot problem.

wet climates. As the mortar deteriorates, water gets in and can rust out the ties, and the bricks begin to fall away. A brick cottage may have kept the big, bad, wolf away, but that's mostly because it was new. Old mortar in bad shape will have a recessed look to it and may have cracks.

A physician I once knew got a bid from a professional mason to clean and repair his brick house. He decided it was too high, and with no training and all the wrong tools, went ahead and did the work himself. He went at it until he had worked his way around the entire house and ground out all the mortar he could reach without a ladder. By the time he was through he'd done so much damage that he couldn't afford to hire the mason to repair it!

Easiest thing to do? Call a mason. This is not a homeowner job. Think of major brick repair the same way you should think of roof replacement; call someone who does it for a living. If you don't want work done right away and your bricks aren't falling out by the truckload, then put off calling the pros.

For a quick and simple temporary repair, you'll need:

- Masonry caulking
- Caulk gun
- Rags

This is not for a permanent repair job, but it's hands down easier than removing old mortar and pointing (applying) new material. Masonry caulk will fill gaps, holes, and cracks in old mortar until you do a more thorough job. It isn't meant for large-scale brick repair, and don't expect it to match the existing mortar. If this doesn't bother you, masonry caulking will get you by until you're ready for the big job.

Masonry caulk is sticky stuff! Apply only a small amount and wipe with a rag dipped in soapy water.

Stuck on Stucco

Stucco cracks, just like interior plaster. The hassle-free approach is to caulk the cracks. You'll need:

- Latex caulk and caulk gun
- Paint brush and water
- Paint

Shoot the caulking into the crack. Then dip an old paintbrush into a small container of water, shake off the excess, and brush the caulk into the crack. This approach works in and spreads the caulk into the uneven surface of the stucco. And it keeps the stuff off your hands! No muss, no fuss, and hardly any time at all! When the caulk is dry, paint it. Use only a minimum of paint, and spread it beyond the caulk with your brush.

YOU'LL THANK YOURSELF LATER

Shrink the job. Break it up into smaller pieces. You don't have to do everything at once. If it's summertime and the weather is good, do 30–45 minutes worth of repairs and touch-ups at a time and go off and enjoy the beach.

Getting Sense on Your Side

The Crazy Way	The Lazy Way
Blithely sand away at lead paint: Hello, lawsuit	Follow the required guidelines: Good Citizen Award
Ignore the extra attention required by the weathered sides of your house	Monitor them, and paint your siding instead of having to replace it
Replace damaged shingles with the wrong grade: Make an unintentional statement against conformity	Match shingle grades properly: Man, I can't even tell where I did the repair
Let paint and siding deteriorate: Paint the whole house	Regularly touch it up and do minor repairs: Good thing we like this color; still looks good
Embarking on a major masonry restoration project yourself: Hey, I had nothing better to do this year	Hire a mason: Best money I ever spent; place looks brand-new
Ignore problems with your LP siding: I like the idea of mushrooms growing out of it	Call the hotline and get the replacement in motion: One big headache out of the way

Windows: Easier Than the Ones on Your Computer

Windows are a house's answer to the ongoing demands for both light and ventilation. It doesn't hurt that they also let you see when your kids are out in the yard playing astronaut and are about to launch a newly found frog they've tied to their kite. Windows are both targets for errant baseballs and our lenses for looking at a Christmas snowfall (Okay, cactus if you're in Arizona).

Like everything else associated with your house, windows come in many flavors: wood, metal, vinyl, aluminum, double-hung, casement, Palladian, and so on. Your main concerns should be:

1. Are they weather-tight?

2. Do they function properly?

In new home construction vinyl windows rule. As with vinyl siding, their life expectancy is a little theoretical—lab conditions don't always duplicate Wyoming wind storms in January—but they are relatively inexpensive and never, ever have to be painted. It doesn't get any better than that!

I Feel Your Pane

Most old homes originally had wood windows. When they're in peak condition, wood windows are beautiful: warm, graceful, highly detailed in some cases. Peak condition lasts as long as the paint or other finish lasts, so vigilance and a paint brush are mandatory with wood windows, even new ones! Many old windows get painted shut over the years or, if painting is neglected, the wood weathers. Repairs can be time consuming.

Older homes often have metal or aluminum windows, the first mass replacements for wood units. These can be in pretty decent shape most of the time—after all, they can't rot and they don't warp easily—but they're often not too effective in the winter since metal alone isn't much of an insulator against cold. Warm air and moisture inside the house collect against the cold glass and metal, making it look like someone turned on a fog machine. Locks and old hand cranking openers are other potential problems with metal windows.

This Old Window

Old houses kept in their original condition are comprised largely of old parts: old doors, old floors, old plumbing, and old windows, to name a few. All of these parts can last indefinitely if maintained, but that can be a big "if."

Originally, most old homes had one of two types of wood windows:

1. Double-hung

2. Casement

Double-hung windows slide up and down. Casement windows open out like a door. Either can need extensive repair work or easy repairs. The latter will get them open and keep them together—all that you really need in order to enjoy your house and your free time.

Problems with old wood windows include:

1. They won't open.

2. The corners are loose or broken.

3. They leak.

To open a double-hung window that's been painted shut you'll need:

- Hammer and putty knife (the stiff-blade type instead of flexible)

- Pry bar

- Silicone spray

YOU'LL THANK YOURSELF LATER

Ninety-nine times out of a hundred the only reason old wood windows won't open is excessive paint build-up. It takes only one negligent paint job, and you're stuck! Follow a few simple steps and you won't be stuck for long.

The 3 Worst Things to Do with Your Old Windows

1. Force open windows that were never meant to open (you'll know this by the lack of pulleys).

2. Get them open, but neglect to replace badly damaged glass.

3. Paint them shut again after going to the trouble of opening them!

(A quick window anatomy lesson. The sash is the part of the window that actually moves; it holds the glass. The sill is the sloped, flat horizontal section at the bottom of the window. It's sloped so it can shed water. The jamb is the frame that holds the sash. End of lesson!)

You can open the window in a few simple steps.

1. Find the areas where the sash touches other parts of the window, that is, where it sits. If these areas are filled with paint, then you know why your window isn't opening! Place your putty knife along these junctions, both inside and out, and lightly tap it with your hammer, breaking any paint bonds.

2. Unlock the window lock.

3. With silicone spray, spray the section of the jamb where the sash will be sliding up. Spray all the areas where you broke the paint with the putty knife, too!

4. Place your putty knife under the lower edge of the sash and the sill, then tap it with your hammer.

5. Take your pry bar and force it under the putty knife. As you tap the bar with your hammer; the sash will start to move up.

6. Force the sash up a bit and then push it back down, slowly working it up and down until it moves freely. Sometimes the bottom section is loose, so watch that it doesn't drop off. Keep spraying with lubricant until it opens freely!

If you touch up your paint, wipe off the silicone. Be sure to move the sash a few times while the paint dries. This is the easy way to keep it working and not get it stuck shut again!

Rope-a-Dope

Most old double-hung windows operate with ropes, pulleys, and sash weights. One end of a rope is connected to the side of the sash and the other is connected to a counterweight inside the wall. The rope passes through a pulley. It's simple and always works, at least until a rope breaks! Replacing a rope can be a hassle, so why not do a hassle-free repair instead? Instead of replacing the rope, you can substitute a piece of hardware. You will need:

- A sash control
- Tin snips or sheet metal shears

A sash control is an inexpensive piece of spring metal—it's actually called a "sash control"— sold in many hardware stores, and is used in place of missing or broken ropes in double-hung windows.

Sometimes, a sash control is too strong; that is, it exerts too much pressure for the sash, and needs to be cut in half lengthwise with a tin snips or sheet metal shears. This will take about another whole minute. A two-minute investment vs. disassembling the window and installing a rope. The lazy choice is pretty clear!

QUICK n' PAINLESS

Two sash controls come in a pack for less than $3. You just open the sash and place the control between the sash and the jamb according to the illustration on the package. It takes less than a minute!

A Case for Casements

Old casements can be a little trickier. After you get them open, the hinges might need replacement or cleaning. The edges are usually caked with paint and caulking. Sometimes they're nailed shut if a former owner had security concerns. With a few tools, you can have them functioning and usable in no time.

To open a painted shut casement window, you'll need a:

- Hammer
- Stiff-blade putty knife
- Pry bar
- Vacuum cleaner
- Spray lubricant

A casement closes against a jamb just like a door closes. At the junction between the sash and jamb, close to the window lock, tap your putty knife in gradually. This will force the casement out slightly.

Continue to do this on all four sides of the sash. On the side opposite the lock, just break the paint. It's the side with the hinges—you don't want to push against those!

After you've broken the paint, tap the putty knife in again near the lock and bend it out a little more aggressively, forcing the sash out further. Continue this up and down the entire side and then at the top and bottom.

Be gentle when you do this! A heavy hand can splinter the sash or jamb. As the sash continues to move outward, you may need the pry bar to help it along. Be sure

YOU'LL THANK YOURSELF LATER

If your casement doesn't close easily, first check the hinges; the screws may be loose. Tighten them completely to pull the sash tight to the jamb.

you push out at the bottom and the top as well. In 10–15 minutes—voilà!—an open window!

Gradually move the sash in and out to work the hinges. Spray them with plenty of lubricant. You'll probably have an assortment of old paint, caulking, dead bugs, and bits of other interesting stuff to clean off and vacuum out. You can scrape the worst of any caulk or paint build-up off the edge of the sash with your putty knife.

If the sash closes tightly, you're done! Stand back and enjoy the fresh air!

Casement II: The Sequel

You've gotten the casement open. Good for you! Many people never get to this point with their old windows. But now it won't close! Don't worry, a speedy solution is at hand. You'll need:

- Small belt sander (3" × 18" belt or smaller)
- One coarse sanding belt and one 100-grit sanding belt
- Dust mask
- Ear protectors
- Vacuum cleaner
- Primer and paint

You'll have to trim one or more edges of the sash for it to close.

Install the coarse sanding belt and run the sander up and down the length of the sash on the lock side. You'll have to lean out a bit to do this. Just sand enough to

A COMPLETE WASTE OF TIME

The 3 Worst Ways to Trim and Adjust a Casement

1. Remove it and run the edges through a table saw.

2. Trim it excessively without testing it for closing tolerances.

3. Ignore excess paint build-up on the jamb and loose hinge screws.

A carpenter will often trim sashes down with a plane, which is a cutting tool designed for shaving and trimming wood. A belt sander does the same thing faster. A small one can be purchased for around $60, and some people can run it comfortably with one hand.

remove any caulk or old paint. Remember, it may be lead-based paint, so do your work according to the guidelines! Close the window. If it still sticks or will not close all the way, look closely and note where you need to do more trimming. Run the sander again, trimming just enough so the sash will close and open easily. Belt sanders work quickly. You'll finish the job before you know it!

Once the sash can open and close, run over it one more time using the 100-grit sanding belt. Vacuum all the dust and paint chips away, prime the sanded areas to seal them up, and paint after the primer has dried. That's it! Mission accomplished!

What's Your Angle?

Wood windows on weathered sides of houses will often deteriorate more quickly than those on more protected sides. When this happens, sometimes the joints at the corners of some window sashes can loosen and begin to separate. Usually this happens at the lower corners. Angle brackets are a quick way to repair these out-of-order corners. To repair a loose corner of a sash, gather together:

- Two galvanized three-inch angle brackets per sash
- One-inch galvanized Phillips wood screws
- Power drill and drill bits
- Screwdriver or Phillips bit for drill

Open the problem sash and push the loose section up as tightly as you can to its original position. If it can't be pushed up all the way, don't worry about it. Place the bracket so it lines up just next to the window putty. Drill a pilot hole (this is the hole you drill before inserting the screw) for one of the bracket's end holes and insert and tighten the galvanized screw. Line up the bracket, drill the remaining holes, screw the bracket tight. Attach the second bracket and your work is finished! A 10-minute task, nothing to it!

There's Something Rotten in Denmark (and Maybe Your Window, Too)

Your sash may be just too far gone for a simple repair. Before you install the brackets, poke around the area with a pocket knife. Does the blade go right through the wood? Is it soft and punky—not in the 1980s pre-grunge music era way, but more like a window with no *there* there—and requiring a lot of specialty rebuilding? If you want the window to open, think about replacing the sash altogether. This can be the easiest approach, and not all that expensive for residential size windows. What do you do next?

1. Look in your phone directory for millwork companies.

2. Give them the approximate size of your sash to get a ballpark replacement price.

3. Ask if they do installations or can recommend an installer to you.

If the price is agreeable, leave this job to someone else. Let the installer take all the measurements! This

YOU'LL THANK YOURSELF LATER

If you do order a new sash, be sure it's primed before it's installed! If possible, have it painted as well, at least on the exterior side. It's much easier to do this before it's in place!

way the problem isn't yours if the measurements are wrong (this happens more often than you might think).

Painless Putty

Putty, or glazing compound, is the white or gray dough-like material that seals the edge of the glass to the wood sash. The glass keeps most of the wind and water outside where it belongs, but the putty keeps smaller amounts from seeping in and rotting out the sash. If you have any putty missing from your windows, it's as simple as frosting a cake to replace it (but do it when the weather is dry). You will need:

- DAP glazing compound
- Putty knife
- Paint

DAP is a brand name glazing compound available at most paint and hardware stores. It always works and has a good consistency. When buying DAP:

1. Buy at least a pint can if you have several windows to do.

2. If you're working in cold weather, warm the can near a heater or by half submerging it in a container of hot water to keep the glazing compound soft.

3. Empty the can and knead the contents until you get a consistency like rubbery bread dough.

Carefully remove any loose, old glazing from your sash. Don't be too aggressive, or you can crack the glass! Brush away any dirt or old, crumbled putty. Knead a racquet-ball size amount of DAP in your hands to soften it further and then force it into the area where the glass meets the sash (some people like to roll the glazing compound into the shape of a snake first). Smooth it over with your putty knife following the angle of the original putty. Put everything away, wash up, and forget about your window for a week while the putty dries and cures.

When the DAP has cured and has a slight "skin" over it, carefully paint it and seal the edge of it to the glass— you'll have to paint over onto the glass just a little. Your job is done and the cruel winds and rain will be kept at bay. Simple maintenance—big results!

Heavy Metal

More often than not, metal and aluminum windows are in pretty decent shape. A shot of WD-40 or silicone once in a while and they're happy. However, unlike wood windows, metal and aluminum are assembled with built-in openers, locks, and internal pulleys that are, in some cases, almost impossible for a homeowner to repair should they break.

The main problem with these windows, aside from hardware breakage, is water seepage. Old metal windows from the wood-window era were held in with metal clips and glazing compound. They can be repaired with new glazing compound as needed, just like an old wood sash.

Older homes usually have metal stops or strips holding in the glass and sometimes water can wash in behind them. The wonderful world of caulk and sealants will rescue you from this problem simply and efficiently. If

IF YOU'RE SO
INCLINED

If you have to patch up any putty on your window, be sure to get it painted after it cures! Many people don't do this and the putty eventually falls out. Painting your new putty is actually the lazy way in the long run.

you're getting seepage with one of your older metal windows, it will probably be at the bottom of a piece of glass, a quick caulking can solve your problem. All you need for the job will be:

- Clear latex caulking
- Caulk gun
- Wet rag
- Razor blade

Locate the area where the seepage is occurring. Dry the area thoroughly. Next to the glass, apply a thin bead of latex clear caulking, taking care that you fill the gap between the metal stop and the glass. Wipe it with a wet, not damp, rag. After it has dried, take your razor blade and clean any smeared material off the glass. During the next rain, check the window for leaks. This is an easy repair and only takes minutes per window. Mark the ones that need caulking and do them all at once! Then, retire that caulk gun for a while and relax!

Do You Take Plastic?

Vinyl windows are another miracle of the petroleum industry. They'll never quite have the panache of wood windows, but they will never, ever need the maintenance, either. New vinyl windows come with hardware attached and weather stripping built in. Spray some silicone on the sliding parts once in a while and your maintenance is done! No, they won't wash themselves, but manufacturers might be working on that!

Congratulations, you now know more about windows than you probably ever wanted to. Do an inventory of your windows and list the tools and materials you'll need. Consider this "fact finding mission" your task for the day, and do the work itself tomorrow!

The Lazy Way

Double-hung vinyl windows that slide up and down may eventually end up with broken spring-wound pulleys or other internal systems built in by their manufacturer to enable the window to move and open. If this happens, take the uncomplicated approach:

1. Call the manufacturer.

2. Tell them the problem.

3. Get the name of someone to call if the company does not do repairs.

Getting Sense on Your Side

The Crazy Way	The Lazy Way
Pry open your window with a screwdriver: Get that dented, distressed look	Break the paint bond first and it opens up in a second
Replace a pane of glass without painting the glazing compound: When it falls out, I'll get more practice	Allowing the glazing compound to cure, then sealing it with paint: It'll stay sealed for years
Break the budget and take the time to replace your repairable wooden windows: Sliding white vinyl looks just dandy on a brick Tudor	Do some simple repairs on the ones you have: Save time and money, and feel too smart for the world
Hold a sash open with a bottle or block of wood instead of replacing the broken ropes with a sash control: Good thing the dog was wearing a hard hat	Open package, slip in control: End of story
Paint your windows shut: There was too much fresh air in here anyway	Move the windows while they dry: Nothing like a summer breeze on a warm night
Use glazing compound right out of the can: Help!	Warm up and knead the compound first: I can't believe how easy this is to apply!

All Decked Out

The first dry day of spring rolls around and you decide to celebrate with a barbecue on your back deck. You think of Fourth of July cookouts: sipping ice-cold beer, smelling fresh-cut grass, wiping tears from your eyes as smoke billowing from illegal fireworks blows your way. You step out to fire up the hibachi and, whoops! You're suddenly skating across a slime-coated deck in less-than-perfect Olympic form. While the judges are posting your scores, you remember that you never did get around to cleaning and sealing the deck last fall.

Decks need some looking after. After spring skidding, you can join in the latest body piercing chic by stabbing your bare feet with splinters.

Most decks are made out of wood, which has a bad habit of trying to relive its days as a tree by soaking up water. Instead of arboreal therapy to convince it that it can't return to its childhood in the woods, you'll need to keep the wood sealed and the water out.

Most deck problems can be avoided with regular cleaning and sealing. Keep the water and fungus out and let the easy times in!

Not sure if your deck is up to snuff? Have it inspected by an experienced carpenter or contractor. You could have major damage. Better to get it repaired before you paint or refinish it, unless you really like practicing your brush strokes!

Care and Feeding

Your job will depend on the condition of your deck or porch.

1. A new deck will be the easiest of all. Just a simple cleaning and sealing once a year will keep it in top shape.

2. An older deck, up to 10 years old, may need a little more help, like an extra cleaning or some minor repairs.

3. If your deck or porch is older than 10 years (especially if it's a much older house), you may need to do more extensive repairs.

   With a little planning, a sound deck in good repair can be yours with simple and hassle-free maintenance.

Giving Your Deck (and Yourself) a Stress Test

Before you clean the deck boards, take a walk around.

1. Is your railing tight or is it wobbly?

2. Are there any nails sticking out?

3. Jump up and down a few times. Does it feel like you should start shopping for earthquake insurance?

4. Poke any suspicious spots with a narrow screwdriver. If it keeps going and going and going through a piece of wood, it's a bad sign.

Bath Time

When decking stops repelling water, it gulps it down. This not only damages the wood, it gives it that slip 'n' slide coating of scum you skate on every spring. Thanks to the wonderful world of chemistry, cleaning scum is a snap.

Deck cleaners act like time machines, that is, while they clean most of the ground-in dirt and taco chips and spilled sodas, they also reverse the discoloration from weathering. Be warned, however, that they cannot undo splintering or other splits in the wood.

To give your deck a bath you'll need:

- Push broom
- Garden hose
- Mop or Scrub brush
- Latex gloves
- Bucket
- Deck cleaner
- Sealer

1 Go to your preferred paint, hardware, or home improvement store and ask for their recommended cleaner. There's always a clerk who's tried one product successfully and can recommend it. If you haven't cleaned the deck in awhile, get an extra gallon of solution.

2 Remove all furniture, plants, small children, and pets.

3 Sweep your deck thoroughly. If your railings look bad, swab them as well.

QUICK n' PAINLESS

Deck cleaners are easy to apply with an old mop. If you have to work the cleaner in, relax and do it with a big push broom. Test a small amount in a corner to determine how long the cleaner should stay on the wood.

4 Follow the directions on the container! If your stains are really tough, rinse with hot water (you can connect your hose to your hot water tap at the washing machine; if it takes two hoses, borrow one from a neighbor).

5 Let the cleaner dry completely before applying the sealer. The sealer is the finish that helps keep rain, snow, and spilled barbecue sauce from shortening the life of your deck.

6 Do any deck cleaning early in the morning before the sun warms up! Too much heat dries out the cleaner, which means more work applying and scrubbing it. Cooler temperatures let you coat larger areas and allow the cleaner to soak in and work longer!

Sorry, Shrink Wrap Won't Do

Before a piece of cedar became part of your backyard fun-in-the-sun American lifestyle, it was part of a cedar tree, protected from the elements by a layer of bark. Strip that away, and it has about as much protection as a Chihuahua has living at the North Pole.

All you have to do to preserve your deck is re-coat it once a year. Decks can be sealed with:

- Paint (not recommended)
- Stain (types vary)
- Clear sealers(good for yearly re-coating)

Paint looks bright and wonderful until it gets water underneath it and begins to lift and peel. You're asking for trouble (and more work!) every time you repaint.

Replacing a deck is a big deal—and a big expense! Your regular cleaning and maintenance shows how smart and fiscally responsible you are—everything your family wanted. Call one of them up and have them take you to dinner in the spare time you now have.

The Lazy Way

Stains will give you some color, but solid-bodied stains have the most pigment. Penetrating stains are clear sealers with some tint thrown in.

Buying and Applying

Purchasing deck sealer and applying it is pretty effortless.

1. Measure the square footage—if you're math-o-phobic, it's the length times the width in feet of your deck—and buy enough sealing material to cover.

2. The clerk who recommended the cleaner can also recommend a sealer specifically made for decks.

3. Clean your deck before sealing.

4. Use a paint roller to apply the sealer—it works great and makes the job go fast! Follow the directions on the can.

When a Bath Just Won't Do

Maybe your deck is a little beyond the clean-only phase. Does it have some splinters, some rough wood, maybe some stains that are staying put like the in-laws that just won't leave? Before you're charged with callous indifference toward the state of your deck, consider sanding.

Sanders

Sanders are one of the electrical tool world's great time-savers. They're noisy and create a lot of dust, and you don't want to use them on your antique piano, but nothing will smooth out rough wood in a hurry like an electric sander.

A COMPLETE WASTE OF TIME

The 3 Worst Things to Do When Applying Sealer

1. Forget to plan ahead (and paint yourself into a corner!).

2. Apply too many coats of sealer.

3. Apply sealer over damp wood.

For most homeowners, a small, compact orbital finishing sander will take care of many jobs. I recommend a Makita finishing sander for its lightweight ease of use and affordable price.

How to Sand with Small Sanders

For finish sanding, you'll need:

- Orbital finishing sander
- Sandpaper
- Extension cord
- Leaf blower
- Dust mask
- Safety glasses
- Ear protectors

1. Always wear safety glasses, a dust mask, and ear protection when sanding.

2. Cut your job down into manageable chunks, say 30 minutes at a time.

3. Sand as many boards as that time allows.

4. Blow the dust off with a leaf blower.

5. Apply the sealer. No need to do any additional cleaning. A few boards a day and the job will go quickly!

If you need something bigger . . .

Pat yourself on the back! The toughest part is getting started and you've done that. Treat yourself to a cold drink and stand back and admire your work!

The Lazy Way

Drum Sanders

Drum sanders can cover large areas of flooring quickly, but require expertise not learned in a single day. These machines are about the size of a lawnmower, but much more powerful! They are the main sanding tool for wood floor installers and refinishers. But if the operator isn't careful, the sander can quickly dig in and gauge wood flooring.

I don't recommend drum sanders for beginners. Unless you are experienced you can easily damage your deck. But if you have a large deck which needs sanding, they can speed up the job. You could hire a floor refinisher to do the job. If you decide to use a drum sander yourself, you should:

1. Hammer down any nail heads sticking up above the decking. Otherwise, they will tear and rip the sandpaper around the drum.

2. Use a light sandpaper, such as 100 grit, at least until you're used to running the machine.

3. Use a finishing sander around the edges and perimeter.

Big Repairs Made Easy

When someone suggests that you loosen up, it might be a good idea for you, but not for your deck. Did you find any loose boards when you did your check-up? Any wobbling? Relax, and enter the grand world of fasteners. Nails and screws will absolve many of your deck's sins.

IF YOU'RE SO
INCLINED

Take a look at your handrails and other sections of your deck. A quick going over with a finish sander and they will look terrific with your newly cleaned decking.

■ Deck screw: A great product available at lumber and hardware stores is the deck screw, a rust-resistant marvel that can secure the most stubborn board. Driven in with a power drill, deck screws can reach deep down and hold wood tight.

■ Galvanized finishing nails: These are nails coated with zinc to resist rusting. They are less expensive than deck screws and work well in many outdoor applications.

Replacing a Rotten Board

Sound intimidating? This is actually manageable by any homeowner. Even if only part of a board is damaged, it's often easier to replace it completely than it is to try to patch it.

Decking is held in by one or two nails (or screws) every 16 inches. A large pry bar makes quick work of removing the offending wood. Does this sound intimidating, too? If you can change a tire, you can pry up a board. Maybe you can convince a handy neighbor to do it since most contractors are too busy for such small jobs.

To replace a rotten board, you'll need:

■ Pry bar

■ Hammer

■ Tape measure

■ Hand saw

■ Galvanized nails or deck screws

■ Electric drill with Phillips bit for deck screws

■ New replacement board

1. Pry up the old board with a pry bar and remove all nails

2. Measure the board (length, width, and thickness!)

3. Purchase a replacement board

4. Cut your new board to length and attach with galvanized nails or deck screws

Repairing Splintered Boards

What if you have some sound, but splintered boards? It's more hassle-free to do a simple repair than to remove the old board, drive to a lumber store, buy new wood, and install it. To repair a splintered, but sound, board you'll need:

- Exterior-Grade carpenter's glue
- Plastic wrap
- A heavy weight
- Orbital finishing sander
- 50-grit sandpaper
- 100-grit sandpaper

1 Liberally brush exterior grade carpenter's glue over the splintered area.

2 Place a piece of plastic wrap on top of the glue.

3 Weight the plastic wrap down—your gallon can of sealer will do nicely—to compress the splintered wood.

4 When dry, sand with a finishing sander. Use 50-grit sandpaper first, then 100-grit during the final sanding.

YOU'LL THANK YOURSELF LATER

Decking materials vary. Some builders use treated lumber, top-grade cedar, or cheaper hemlock. Tell your supplier what you're using the replacement wood for to get the best material for your deck.

5 After the repair is done, dry, and sanded, you need to re-seal the area with the same sealer you used on the rest of the decking surface.

You could try repairing splintered boards with exterior Spackle.

Every time it rains, you might get the opportunity to repair it again when the Spackle lifts off!

Plywood Decks

Plywood decks form a solid deck surface that must be kept sealed and protected even more than individual decking boards. Plywood will delaminate if exposed to rain and snow and can be tough to repair.

Unlike all those individual decking boards, plywood lies flatter and doesn't pull up as easily, so less nailing for you! And you can roll the finish on in a jiffy with a paint roller. Nothing is easier to roll paint onto than a flat floor.

Coatings for Plywood

Paint is not a good sealant for plywood decks. Here, we enter the world of exotic, and toxic, polysyllabic coatings. Some, like elastomeric, are like liquid rubber, and come in two parts: the undercoat and the tinted sealer or top coat. These are the kinds of finishes archaeologists in A.D. 2700 will find still intact. However, the sealer, or top coat, does have to be reapplied from time to time, although not as often as stains, clear sealers, or paint. If you're uncomfortable with the idea of applying a finish that requires you to wear a respirator, you may want to hire this one out (let's just say I'd suggest it).

A two-foot section of decking can be glued and sanded in less than 10 minutes. While the glue is drying, relax in your hammock and read some of that novel you've been meaning to get around to!

The Lazy Way

Concrete, Brick, or Stone—the Easiest Yet!

They're not exactly decks, but concrete patios, brick terraces, and stone gardens serve the same purpose. Best of all, you can maintain them with one hand tied behind your back. Just rinse regularly with a hose while you're out watering the garden. If mildew is a problem, you'll need:

- Garden hose
- Household bleach
- Liquid detergent
- Scrub brush
- Mixing bucket
- Old mop

1 Mop thoroughly with a mix of water and household bleach (3:1 ratio) and let it sit a few minutes.

2 Rinse with a hose or pressure washer.

3 If some stubborn dirt or stains remain, scrub with a mild household soap (you don't want to kill any plants!) using a push broom.

The Porch—Your Outdoor Living Room

A porch, like a deck, is another outdoor room, except that a ceiling and solid floor make it a little more civilized.

Having an outdoor floor made up of individual floor boards is usually asking for trouble, but a porch can get away with it because the floor is mostly sheltered and covered.

Potted plants and wood planters can leave stains on concrete just as they do on wood. Move them periodically—change is a good thing anyway—and clean any spots under them before they get tough to remove.

QUICK n' PAINLESS

Don't like the looks of those tattered boards? Throw a large, industrial, rubber-backed outdoor mat over them (but pick it up once in a while in case any water gets underneath it, then allow it to dry out). The mat will cover an ugly spot and keep the wood protected.

Mostly, but not quite. Usually, the area at the top of the steps gets the most wear and tear. The floor boards get worn and they split, the ends of the boards deteriorate, and the paint is more likely to chip or peel. To really clean it up, you would have to strip and sand the boards, patch any deteriorated areas with an epoxy filler or something similar like liquid fiberglass. Then prime and repaint. A lot of work, not to mention the problem of sanding lead-based paint!

The Painless Porch Exam

Your porch should get a once-a-year check-up just like your deck. Be sure to look for:

- Rot
- Loose floor boards
- Deteriorated paint
- Wasp, yellow jacket, or other insect nests in the ceilings.

Insects

If you see any of these less-than-benign creatures flying out of a hole the size of a dime, don't plug the hole! They must be exterminated or removed. If you're uncomfortable with spraying the nest, call an exterminator who will guarantee the work.

An exception should be made for bees. Normally, an exterminator can recommend someone who can remove them from your porch and install them in a legitimate beehive.

Loose Boards

Most loose porch boards are on the steps. Stand on each step and shift back and forth on your feet. If you get too much movement in a board:

1. Secure it with galvanized finishing nails or screws.

2. Fill nail or screw holes with wood patch.

3. Sand when patches are dry.

4. Prime and touch up with matching paint.

Rot

Rot can occur under the porch, especially if there isn't much ventilation. Fungi like to get funky where it's damp and dark. If you've got access to the space under your porch, you'll need:

- Flashlight or emergency light

- Narrow screwdriver or pocket knife

- Old clothes

1. Take a flashlight or emergency light and crawl in. Be prepared for some spiders!

2. With a screwdriver or pocket knife, poke around at any wood close to the ground, especially posts.

3. If the screwdriver sinks in and the wood breaks away easily, have a contractor come and look at your porch.

4. Remove any dirt that may be banked up against any piece of wood. Be sure to check the wood for rot or damage.

Got the board replaced? Practice your Irish jig on it to check for soundness. If the neighbors give you a weird look, take a bow.

The Lazy Way

When to Consider a Contractor

Do things look bad? Is one end of your porch way lower than the other? Can you tell a pry bar from a high bar? Call a reputable contractor and get an estimate for repairs or replacement. Come home and relax on your porch swing after the work is done!

Getting Sense on Your Side

The Crazy Way	The Lazy Way
Let your deck take care of itself: You'll need care when you skid and break your leg	Clean and seal the deck every fall: It'll stay safe and sound for years
Use a drum sander if you're inexperienced: It'll take ages to replace all the boards you gouged	Choose an orbital finishing sander: These are the good times!
Patch deck boards	It takes half the time replace them entirely
Paint your deck: Hello, rotten boards!	Use a strong sealant now and then: Get decades of wear
Sand the paint off a deck made from inferior or rotting wood	Find out if the wood is good before you take time to sand it; if not, replace it
Leave porch steps loose: Lose time when your neighbor takes you to court	Examine your porch steps once a year and secure or replace them

Chapter

twelve

It's All Downhill: Easy Yard Maintenance

If you're a downtown city dweller, your yard consists of a potted herb sitting near your kitchen window up on the 20th floor of your co-op. For some would-be farmer suburbanites, a yard might be two or more acres of lawn that Dad mows every Saturday, sitting high atop a Sears tractor mower and entertaining agrarian fantasies of "working the land." Personally, I don't know of any farmers who harvest crops of Scott's All-Turf Lawn Mix.

Yards serve several purposes. They do provide us with a link to the land, even if it is a sanitized connection. A yard provides some distance from neighbors and furnishes us with some privacy. Kids, when they're not glued to TV screens or computer monitors, may actually still use yards for playing, at least when they're little. When they get older, they sense that yards have stopped being play areas and have become sites upon which Calvinistic retribution (mowing the lawn and raking the leaves) is exacted by church elders (in the form of their parents) for the fact that they once enjoyed themselves there.

As a homeowner, the crucial decision you have to make about your yard is, are you going to emphasize grass or landscaping? Landscaping involves a lot of work and expense. Grass involves, well, grass and a few plants here and there that can take care of themselves, such as evergreens.

Happiness is a Lawn Chair, Not a Lawnmower

The easiest way to take care of a yard that's all or mostly lawn? Hire it out!

Mowing the lawn is a thankless task. Does anyone really want to do it? Or have they simply succumbed to the social pressure of doing as their neighbors do? If you don't want to look like the neighborhood bum, short of trying to convince everyone that you're part of a University of Wyoming 10-year study on the potential for prairie development in urban areas, you'll probably have to keep the green stuff cut one way or another.

Hire it out.

There is never a shortage of licensed, relatively cheap landscaping companies who will mow your lawn on a regular basis. Set a schedule and, generally, a crew will show up in a massive truck full of mowers and blowers and trimmers. They will descend upon your yard, communicating telepathically, each crew member armed with a machine to cut or trim or blow grass clippings out of your yard and out of your life. In a matter of minutes, they're gone. You'll leave for work in the morning and come home to a trim, socially acceptable lawn, the envy of the neighborhood.

Unless you cut grass for a living or derive some therapeutic value from it, it's a rather ridiculous activity. You can never stay ahead of it—grass is growing even while you're mowing it! You can't eat it like you could a real food crop, unless you're trying some new reduced-fat bovine diet. It demands attention, food, and water. If you fertilize it, it grows even faster. It's a vicious cycle. In some parts of the country where water availability is now being scrutinized, lawns are being torn out in favor of native landscaping, like rocks and cactus. They don't even have to be watered!

If you're going to hire a landscaping company to do the mowing:

1. Be sure they are licensed and bonded.

2. Get two or three written bids.

3. Agree to the work you want done.

4. Agree in writing to the frequency of the mowing and the fees.

At a time when litigation has become a national pastime, hiring an unlicensed individual to mow your lawn could land you in the position of being legally responsible as an employer for any injuries the person may sustain while mowing your lawn. Even if the person is hurt while using his or her own lawnmower, you could get caught in the middle of some hospital bills. If nothing else, you could end up with your own Lawnmowergate

IF YOU'RE SO
INCLINED

We torture grass when we cut it too short. Many grasses grow to a natural height of over 12 feet. Check with your local agricultural extension service to find out the best height and recommended fertilizer for your lawn.

and be subject to paying someone else's social security taxes if the IRS ever audits that person. Gone are the days when you could safely hire the enthusiastic teenage entrepreneur who offered to cut the lawn and rake up. And gone are the enthusiastic teenagers.

Bids will vary, so get two or three of them. Someone new to the business, especially someone new to the country, may charge less in order to build up a business and referrals. Mowing the lawn isn't exactly nuclear science, so a low price may not indicate lower quality.

Sometimes, lawn mowing can become like carpet cleaning: a cheap basic price, but, oh, we really should fertilize, spray for pest control, spread some lime, reseed, and so on. You may well want some of these services, but be prepared to pay for them. They may result in a more perfect lawn than you really need unless you expect the PGA tour to stop by and practice their putting.

How often do you want your lawn cut? Once a week? Once a month? If you absolutely hate the idea of mowing your lawn and, likewise, absolutely hate the idea of paying for it, stretch it out as long as you're willing to be the neighborhood outlaw. This will depend on the climate you're in, the type of grass you have, and its growth rate. For many lawns, you might get away with once every three weeks.

If you have a very small lawn, the so-called postage stamp size, buy yourself a hand mower and have at it. The mower will last for years, will never need gasoline, oil, or tune-ups, and you'll never disturb the neighbors with a noisy power mower. It may not be worth hiring such a small job out because the cost may not be commensurate with the job. A hand mower is an uncomplicated, quiet approach that's both stress- and hassle-free.

Escaping Landscaping

The traditional English garden is an attempt to bring order and table manners to the rude, boorish world of plants and dirt. Monet's garden was a piece of art. The hanging gardens of Babylon were a wonder of the ancient world. Your yard could be just like any of them if you had the same cheap labor to sustain and maintain them.

Cheap lawn mowing is one thing. True yard maintenance is something else. Weeding, pruning, planting, transplanting—all of these labors will cost more than lawn mowing if you decide to hire them out. If not, you have to decide if you want your yard to look like Monet's, or more like the guy's who sells velvet paintings out of his van at the weekend flea market. His yard is probably a lot simpler.

The Ivy Leagues

Would you rather spend your time weeding or sail boarding? Pruning or hanging out at a bookstore on a Sunday afternoon? These decisions will determine how easy your yard maintenance will be!

If you like gardening, if you see your yard as a blank canvas to be filled from a palette of gardenias, roses, and tulips, skip this section and go back to your gardening books. Your yard is a source of pleasure, delight, and

QUICK ⬛ PAINLESS

If the idea of a hand mower doesn't appeal to you, try an electric weed trimmer for really small areas of grass. Lightweight, fast, and low maintenance, a "weed whacker" will speed up the job!

inspiration. However, if your yard is just another thing you have to deal with, and you'd like to do so with the least possible amount of work and still get some decent results, think ground cover (other than grass). Think evergreens.

Flowers grow in dirt. Shrubs, bushes, and vines grow in dirt. Unfortunately, weeds call dirt home, too, so the more you can fill your garden beds and yard with competing plants, the less space for weeds. More plants equal more work. Who wants that? The easy solution is a fast-spreading, low-maintenance ground cover. These would include:

- Ivy (different types)
- Pachysandra
- Various herbs

Your local climate and soil will determine the ground cover most suited to your yard. To find out what's appropriate for your area:

1. Visit the largest local nursery near you and inquire.

2. Check with gardening clubs.

3. Investigate university extension services.

Local nurseries will not only be able to make recommendations, but will have many types of ground cover available. Look over the stock carefully. Sometimes a smaller nursery may have a better tended selection than, say, a general home improvement center.

Buy plenty of your chosen ground cover! At least an entire flat of it. The more the merrier if you're trying to cover an area quickly. Plant it as early in the season as you can so it can start its "cover up" as soon as possible.

You want your plants to grow and spread quickly so they can start kicking out the weeds before they get started. Buy the fastest-growing variety you can.

Be sure your choice will do well in your climate and the conditions of your yard. Will it grow in direct sunlight? Shade? What about soil with poor drainage? All these conditions will affect your selection, so be sure to account for them when making your purchase. You only want to plant once and to make that as uncomplicated as possible.

Gardeners love to talk shop. A garden club may have a member who would assist you in your decisions and make recommendations. I wouldn't necessarily mention that you're just trying to cover up your yard so it can take care of itself, though. Gardeners can be very serious people who may not understand your lack of interest in the different varieties of grape hyacinth.

Universities will sometimes have agricultural or horticultural extension services that offer information on planting and local crops and gardens. A few phone calls may uncover a wealth of material.

Massive ground cover does not necessarily exclude planting flowers or shrubs. It just means that eventually you can choke out many of the weeds by doing nothing but watering your garden. The idea is that your English ivy prevail over the dandelions. A tenacious ground cover won't eliminate every weed, but it can cut down on most of them, giving you the free time to sit in the sun instead of toiling in it!

IF YOU'RE SO
INCLINED

Trees add value and beauty to most yards. Consider planting some flowering fruit trees or dogwoods. Plant them far enough from the house so their leaves stay out of your gutters. A one-time planting and some occasional care on your part will pay big rewards!

Evergreens are another time saver. If you want to fill some space, pop in some mungo pines and stand back. Even the dwarf variety is no shrinking violet. Evergreens are often like the Eveready bunny: They just keep growing and growing and growing. They are generally undemanding and often forgiving about not being watered regularly. They grow in some variety or another from the East Coast to the Pacific Northwest.

Don't they need some maintenance? Sure, but not much. Just trim them down to size when they start to get out of hand. Practice your artistry on them and turn them into sculptures of popular political figures. Your guests could be greeted by Richard Nixon on one side of your front door and Lyndon Johnson on the other. You could line your driveway with game show hosts, or maybe the Rolling Stones. The possibilities abound, and you'll undoubtedly endear yourselves to the neighbors.

Don't like evergreens? Make the same inquiries about alternative plantings, such as shrubs, as you would about ground covers. Find out what grows best—and quickest—in your area. Shrubs and other bushy plants that feature both berries and flowers can be especially attractive and make good fillers in barren garden areas.

A yard can be a hobby or a prison. If you don't want to devote all your free time to it during the warmer months, plant it as simply as possible, fill it with ground cover, and hire out the lawn mowing.

YOU'LL THANK YOURSELF LATER

If you want to fill some large gaps in the yard fast, ask your nursery for the largest and fastest-growing shrubs available. Plant them where it will be years before you'll have to prune them. Then lay around in your hammock and watch them grow.

Getting Time on Your Side

	The Old Way	The Lazy Way
You mowing the lawn vs. Lucy's Lawnmowing Ladies mowing the lawn	All morning	How long to write a check?
Weeding the beds vs. filling them with ground cover	Perpetually	Plant once, and walk away from it
If you're in a desert area, going natural vs. trying to have a yard like a Scottish golf course	Forever	Rake the sand once a year
Bagging grass and clippings vs. using a mulching mower	Every time you mow	What bags?
Building a fence and painting it every few years vs. planting a hedge	Hope you have free weekends	Plant once, walk away from it
Pulling dandelions vs. making dandelion wine	How many you got?	A little longer, but tastier!

Power Plays and Pipe Dreams: Keep Your Lights Glowing and Your Water Flowing

Electrical wiring and plumbing, together with heating and air conditioning, make up a house's operating system. Flip a switch, open a tap, or plug in a hair dryer and the system responds with power or water to keep us warm, light our way, or help us wash the clothes. We easily take these systems for granted because they mostly work day after day without delays or problems. Still, a little ignorance is worse than a little knowledge, so a tour of these systems and some suggested maintenance is in order.

You need permits from your local building department to add circuits or, usually, even to add to an existing circuit. Don't short circuit yourself, and maybe your house, by doing work without proper permits. Inspectors are there to ensure the work is done safely and properly.

ALL SYSTEMS GO!

For most practical purposes, all you need to know about electricity (beyond not to stick your fingers in sockets) is:

1. How to inspect your current system.

2. How to avoid overloading or shorting a circuit.

3. That you must always shut off the power to a circuit if you're replacing a receptacle, switch, or light.

4. How to shut off the power.

If your house is new, the whole system would have been inspected by your local building department and should be in good shape. (This isn't always true, however, sometimes problems are missed.) If you're not having any problems, don't worry about it. A home built after the 1940s will be more up-to-date than an old home, but should still be looked over.

An old home might have a system that Ben Franklin would have been proud to install. These systems can be the most precarious if they've been added to or altered over the years.

Plug Away

With an old electrical system, it's a good idea to know where you stand. Typically, the previous owners poked and probed and tinkered with the place and added an outlet or two, maybe a new bathroom light.

In an old house, the original installation of knob-and-tube wiring was usually done very professionally.

Remember, electricity was still pretty new back then, and electricians weren't interested in building reputations as de facto arsonists. At junctions, wires were twisted together, soldered, and then wrapped with tape. They weren't taking any chances! There's no guarantee that any additions to your wiring were done as conscientiously, so you should give them an inspection.

To inspect, you'll need:

- Circuit tester
- Small notebook and pen

A circuit tester is an inexpensive probe available at most hardware stores. It has two wires, joined at a plastic junction that houses a small light bulb. Each wire has a metal prong at its end which you insert into outlets and light fixtures to test for electrical current.

You can also test outlets for grounding, that is, that the current makes a point of returning to the panel or fuse box and ultimately to the earth outside via a separate wire. This means its potential for harm, i.e., electrocution, is minimized. If it doesn't make this return trip, you may end up being the conductor on the electricity train, which isn't such a hot idea.

You'll want to test all of your outlets. To test:

1. Insert both probes, one for each vertical slot, into the outlet.

2. Check that the probe's light bulb is lighted.

3. In your notebook, mark that the outlet is functioning.

QUICK ⬛ PAINLESS

Inspecting your electrical system doesn't take long, and will help you or your electrician solve problems much more quickly.

It's unlikely that an old system is grounded. While you're testing the outlets, test for grounding, too:

1. Insert one probe in one vertical slot of the outlet.

2. Touch the other probe to the screw that holds the plastic or metal cover plate over the outlet.

3. If the bulb does not light up, try the other vertical slot.

4. In your notebook, record whether the outlet is grounded or not.

This inspection is pretty effortless and will provide you and an electrician with useful information.

Don't Blow Your Fuse

Old wiring systems work fine if our demand on them doesn't exceed what they were designed to carry, usually an outlet or two per room and a ceiling light. But then we added computers, stereo systems, and turbo-max self-driving vacuum cleaners, and wonder why the fuses keep frying. Simple, all of these toys demand more current than some circuits are designed to carry. Like the little engine that could, the wiring still tries to do the job, but eventually a fuse notices that things are heating up a little too much and breaks off the relationship. That's the purpose of a fuse or a circuit breaker, to disrupt the current in a circuit before the wire overheats and starts a fire.

Every circuit in a house is designed to allow only a certain number of players to use it—so many lights, so many small items like clock radios, an electric range—and these restrictions should be respected. Every fuse or circuit breaker represents one circuit. How do you know what each fuse controls? First:

1. Find your fuse box.

2. Open the cover door.

3. Look for a list of fuses and their circuits.

Often these lists are incomplete or outdated. The original electrician may have marked fuses that controlled the kitchen, bathroom, and bedrooms. Any additional wiring done over the years may not have been accurately recorded. It's a good idea to write up a new, accurate list and post it on the door of the fuse box. The easiest way to do this is to:

1. Turn on everything in the house.

2. Be sure every outlet has something small plugged into it, such as a lamp or radio.

3. Post a friend or relative in each room.

4. Start unscrewing the fuses one at a time.

5. Note which rooms or sections of the house are affected when each fuse is loosened.

6. Write up your new list and leave a copy on the fuse box door.

In really big houses, this can be a lot of fun, especially if someone did some really weird remodeling over the years. But unlike the buzz you might get from the Electro-Shock Grip of Death machine at a carnival fun house, real electricity is no laughing matter. Even

QUICK ∎ PAINLESS

Is your old circuit list looking like a Dead Sea Scroll? Even if it's current, print up a new one. Add some extra lines for future changes.

changing a fuse should be done cautiously. To change or loosen a fuse safely:

1. Stand on a dry floor. Put a board under your feet if necessary.

2. Use only one hand and keep your other hand away from the fuse box.

3. Touch only the outer rim of the fuse!

4. Never change a fuse in the dark (keep a flashlight nearby).

5. Use only replacement fuses with the same amp rating.

If you have both hands on or near the fuse, there is a chance that you'll become part of an errant current, so this really is a job you can and should do with one hand tied behind your back! If you're really concerned, some electrical supply houses sell special plastic tongs for loosening fuses.

Let There Be Light

Now you know where the fuse box is located and what area each fuse controls. The next time you blow a circuit, you'll be on top of the situation. Your job will be easier, though, if you can avoid blowing or shorting a fuse altogether!

Fuses blow for one of two reasons: shorts or overloads.

A short occurs when the current doesn't follow the plan and decides to head back to the panel box or ground via a short-cut. This usually happens when a bare wire touches another bare wire or a piece of metal. Electricity, being undisciplined and not all that intelligent, figures this is a faster way home and runs for it. Unfortunately, this bit of acting out can result in a shock to you or possibly even a fire in your house.

Sometimes it isn't the circuit that's the problem, but something you've got plugged into it that's causing the short. How do you find out? Simple elimination. Follow these easy steps:

1. Check all the outlets and switches for black smudge marks.

2. Inspect all cords and plugs on lamps and any appliances using the circuit.

3. Check that you haven't just overloaded the circuit.

If you don't find any of the above problems, you'll need to:

1. Disconnect everything from the circuit, and shut off all the light switches.

2. Install a new fuse. If it blows immediately, your problem is in the wiring itself.

3. Turn on the lights one at a time. If the fuse blows, the short is in the switch or in the light fixture you switched on when the fuse blew.

4. If it isn't in a light fixture or switch, then unscrew the fuse, and plug in the lamps or appliances one at a time, tightening the fuse each time. Unscrew the fuse before plugging in the next item and then tighten it again.

QUICK n' PAINLESS

You know what an overload is—too much stuff trying to run at once on one circuit. Run fewer appliances and lights on the circuit you keep overloading and the problem is solved painlessly!

A COMPLETE WASTE OF TIME

The 3 Worst Ways to Act
Around Electricity

1. Not think of it as a fire
   hazard.

2. Knowingly overload
   the circuits.

3. Use outlets that are
   broken or cracked.

5. If the fuse blows, either that lamp or appliance is the problem, or the outlet itself. It could also be that you have eventually plugged in one too many items that are demanding more power than the circuit can provide.

6. If you think it's the lamp or appliance, install a new fuse and plug a different item into the outlet. If the fuse holds, you can be sure the problem is in the lamp or appliance plugged in earlier, not in the outlet.

With old systems, preventive maintenance works best. To avoid problems, you should:

1. Never overload a circuit.

2. Spread the load. Don't run a stereo, TV, computer, and other toys all in the same room.

3. Limit your use of extension cords. Never use them as permanent wiring.

4. Don't replace fuses with larger amp fuses to avoid overloading the circuit. You'll do just the opposite!

5. Limit your use of converter plugs that allow appliances with three-pronged plugs to be plugged into two-pronged outlets.

If you follow these practices you can use your old system without taxing it. If you have any misgivings, an inspection by a licensed electrician is also a good idea.

Pulling a Switch

Fuses and circuit breakers are housed in service panels. Each panel has a main disconnect—the big guy that will shut down all the power in your house. If you need to pull the switch, be sure you have a flashlight with you so you can find your way back out afterward!

Why would you ever shut the power off? Emergencies, such as what looks like fireworks shooting out of your stove, is one reason you might do this. In such a panicked moment, you may not be able to find the fuse or breakers specifically for the stove, so it's better to shut off all the power.

Time to Drop a Dime

You may find that your system just isn't up to snuff for the way you want to live. You don't want to have to keep your stereo turned off while you run your three gigabyte hard drive PC, but you don't want to play with fire either. You just want your wiring to work. Call an electrician, but be prepared for a different kind of shock.

Upgrades and new systems cost money. The best approach, and, in the end, the easiest, is to install a new service—a shiny, up-to-code service panel with circuit breakers instead of fuses—and bring at least some of the house up to code. Discuss your options with your electrician. You can rewire areas of immediate concern, such as the kitchen, bathroom, and laundry and add more circuits later. Existing lights and outlets for small items like clock radios and floor lamps can normally be left alone.

IF YOU'RE SO
INCLINED

Take a tour of your service panel so you'll know how to shut the power off before you have an emergency. Your panel may be controlled by a lever, or a single circuit breaker. Now you'll be ready for action if and when the time comes.

Hot Stuff

Knob-and-tube wiring was used into the 1940s when multi-conductor cable was introduced. It contains both the hot and the neutral wires. If this is what you've got in your home, don't mess with it! The insulation it's wrapped in doesn't age very gracefully and can be very brittle.

Another new, improved wiring method was BX cable, a metal sheathing wrapped around the wiring. It also has a problem with getting old and, if you're experiencing unexplained electrical shorts, should be looked at by a professional electrician.

Some older homes may have polarized receptacles, which are commonly used now. Look at the plug at the end of a lamp or radio or kitchen appliance and you'll notice that the prongs are two different sizes. These plugs help maintain the continuity of the circuit and offer some protection against shock.

Plugged In

The wiring in new houses is great. Everything up to code, grounded outlets everywhere (those are the ones that take three-pronged plugs), circuit breakers in the panel box, and plenty of power. What's to maintain? If you're not experiencing any problems, and you shouldn't be if your wiring was installed and inspected properly, it's just plug and go, right? Well, just about. You have one minor, less-than-a-minute chore to do once a month: the GFI check.

A GFI is a ground-fault interrupter, a special receptacle required in kitchens, bathrooms, and outdoors. Why? Because it can sense small changes in an electrical current and shuts down the power immediately when things go awry. What kind of changes? The ones that occur when you're standing in a puddle outdoors or in your bathtub and decide to plug something, anything, into a nearby outlet. Standing in water is an open invitation for electricity to hop out and see what's going on, using you as an observation post. A GFI senses this and shuts down before you light up like the golden arches.

To ensure that your GFI (sometimes called a GFCI, or ground-fault circuit interrupter) stays happy and alert, it should be tested monthly. All you need to do is:

1. Press the black test button.

2. Watch the red reset button pop out.

3. Press the reset button in and test again in another month.

If the reset button does not pop out, you probably have a faulty GFI and it should be replaced immediately! This is a small job for an electrician, but worth paying for if you are not comfortable doing the replacement yourself. In the meanwhile, you're better off not using the outlet.

TAPPING IN

Despite the comments of certain nags who drink only bottled water (which isn't always as clean or pure as they may think), municipally supplied water is a wonder, and

QUICK 🔲 PAINLESS

Check all of your appliances, lamps, and stereo cords and plugs. Are any of them frayed? Is the plastic casing around the prongs cracked? Are the prongs loose? If so, find someone through a neighborhood hardware store who will do the repair work for you.

To find the main shut-off:

1. Find your water meter near the street or sidewalk.

2. Trace the path from the meter to your house.

3. Follow the main water supply pipe coming from the water meter into your house, and locate the valve.

4. After you've found it, if it's hard to turn, squirt it with Liquid Wrench Super Penetrant to be certain it will work when you need it.

something we all take for granted. We use it for everything: hygiene, cooking, washing our imported car of choice, and survival. Turn on the tap and a seemingly endless supply of the stuff comes gushing out.

As with everything else in your house, the age of your plumbing will tell you something about it.

Going with the Slow

Galvanized pipes were the tubes of choice until copper took over in the late 1950s. Unlike copper, galvanized pipes can corrode and deteriorate, especially if the local water supply isn't galvanized-friendly.

If you have galvanized pipes and suffer from slow water flow, unless it's a problem with the city pipes, you're pretty much stuck with it. Once a pipe in your house has corroded there's less room inside for water to flow. Until someone comes up with a plumber's version of angioplasty, there's no practical way to clean corrosion out of water pipes. Drain lines are another matter. These can be cleaned and easily maintained.

Water, Water Everywhere

Just as important as getting water to run is knowing how to shut it off! Shutoff valves are really important. I mean, really important. The first time a pipe bursts from freezing weather, you'll be glad you know where the main shutoff valve is located. Water damage can be a lot more expensive than repairing the pipe.

Your house has two types of shutoffs:

1. The main shutoff valve

2. Individual shutoffs

The main shutoff is the big guy that shuts off everything. In new homes, it's located inside the house or garage and is marked "Main Water Supply Shutoff Valve" or something to that effect.

In older homes, the main shutoff valve could be located in the basement or laundry room or garage. It may not be clearly marked, so you'll have to do some investigating.

Mark the shutoff valve with a big hanging tag and let a responsible housemate know where it is, too. It may have to be turned off sometime when you're not around.

Old houses sometimes have shutoffs located outside. They often look like an L-shaped metal rod sticking out of the ground. These things are ancient! If you have one, test it to be sure it hasn't turned stiff from rust or corrosion.

Individual shutoffs are usually located at the washing machine, toilets, and sinks. These valves are located under the sinks and toilets and behind the washing machine. Why are they here? To make your life simple if you ever have to repair a single fixture. It's child's play to turn them off, and beats hunting around for the main shutoff.

Your old house may not have these individual shutoffs. If that's the case, be sure you know where the main shutoff is located and that it works properly. It's the only shutoff you've got!

If your water flow is a little slow but you can live with it, leave it alone! Start budgeting for future plumbing replacement now, then relax in a gentle shower.

The Lazy Way

Take It Away!

Each fixture has a drain line. Each drain line empties into the main drain or main stack. This empties into a sewer or septic tank. It's kind of like every drain along the way dumps its problem in another drain's lap until it disappears—not unlike how some government agencies work.

Keep your drains clear and your water-related life will be smooth sailing. Let them get clogged and you'll be sinking in the mire (and looking for a plumber to hire). It won't take any elbow grease to keep the grease and gunk out of your drains. Some ways to manage drains:

1. Use drain strainers if your drains will accommodate them.

2. Avoid putting coffee grounds, tea leaves, fats, or fibrous vegetables down your kitchen drain.

3. Run plenty of hot water as a final rinse after the drain water is gone.

4. Collect food grease in a yogurt container and toss it in the trash.

There are plenty of old-fashioned preventive remedies for drains, too, such as:

Pour one cup of baking soda down each drain, then pour one cup of white vinegar over the baking soda. Finally, let sit for 30 minutes and flush with very hot water.

You can pour in boiling water if the fixture is steel or porcelain. Don't try it with one-piece vanity/sink combinations! If you pour boiling water on them, you can crack the finish! Unlike some commercial drain cleaners, baking soda and vinegar break down grease and fats in a benign manner without affecting your pipes.

For grease build-up, you'll need:

1. One pound of washing soda

2. Three gallons of boiling water

Mix and pour down slow draining drains. A kettle of boiling water once a week or more in each appropriate drain does wonders!

A large volume of water can also help keep your drains clear, and it's painless! Once a week (or more often, if you want):

1. Put the stopper in your drain and fill the sink with hot, soapy water.

2. When full, remove the stopper.

The weight and volume of water helps push along any reluctant bits of gunk before they can make a permanent home in your drain line. A quick wipe with a rag after the water is gone and your sink will be cleaner, too!

Take the Plunge

There are plungers and there are plungers. If you have running water, you should have a plunger around the house. A flanged plunger forms a better seal than a standard cup plunger. For those drains that won't accommodate the flange, simply tuck the flange section up and inside the cup portion of the plunger end. This will give you a flat surface for drains that require it.

QUICK n' PAINLESS

The next time you make a cup of tea, fill the kettle and pour the excess boiling water down the kitchen drain. Put another kettle of water on while you relax with your tea. Pour the second kettle full down the tub drain. Take a load off your drains and your feet!

Sometimes your drain may be beyond the vinegar and soda remedy, like when you toss one too many tossed salads into the kitchen disposal. Usually, the entire drain isn't the problem, just the trap under the sink or tub. A trap is the bent, curved section of pipe which, true to its name, traps a small amount of water to act as a barrier to any sewer gases which would otherwise seep up the waste pipe and into your life. They can also trap food, hair, grease, and small toys.

The easiest way to clear this kind of minor blockage is with a plunger. To do so:

1. Place the plunger over the top of the drain.

2. Push down slowly, forcing out any air from under the plunger.

3. Pull up hard. The vacuum created should clear the blockage.

4. Repeat several times if necessary.

If you have to take the plunge with a bathroom sink or tub, stuff a piece of plastic in the overflow hole (usually below or across from the faucet) to ensure a good vacuum will be created. Once the drain line is clear, run very hot water into it for several minutes.

One thing to remember: never use a plunger if you've poured commercial drain cleaner down the drain. Use one or the other, but not both. The drain cleaner can come spraying out in the direction of the plunger operator!

YOU'LL THANK YOURSELF LATER

Does your sink seem to be draining just a bit slowly, almost unnoticeably? Take the plunger to it anyway. It won't hurt anything, and can prevent a bigger problem later.

Drain Brains

Two general types of commercial drain cleaners are available: caustic and enzyme-based. The latter are environmentally benign and apparently marginal in results. The caustic variety of cleaners will do the job, but should be used in limited applications when clearing old steel drain lines. Although plastic drain lines are inert to these chemicals, use them only if a plunger fails to do the job.

Everyone's Throne

Toilets in the modern sense have been around since the 19th century. They have begotten singing toilet seats, designer toilet paper, and the varying methods of toilet training. When used as their design intended, they're certainly preferable to any alternatives, like backyard outhouses.

Some simple, easy "toilet training" includes:

1. Keeping the lid closed so nothing drops in that's not supposed to drop in (like small toys).

2. Checking the seal between the toilet and the floor for leaks.

3. Checking for leakage where it attaches to the bowl.

Plungers work wonders with plugged toilets. They're an easy, low-tech approach for clearing obstructions. Whatever you do, don't keep flushing once you find the water isn't going anywhere. Bring in the plunger!

The same steps apply for toilets as for sinks:

1. Be sure you have a good seal between the plunger and the opening at the bottom of the toilet bowl.

A COMPLETE WASTE OF TIME

The 3 Worst Things to Do to Your Toilet

1. Stand on it to change the ceiling light bulb.

2. Flush anything down it except modest amounts of paper products.

3. Pour boiling water into it.

2. Push down slowly, forcing the air out from under the plunger.

3. Pull up and let the vacuum action do the work.

4. Repeat as necessary.

If your toilet seems to be gradually taking longer to do its business, take a plunger to it before it gets any worse. If that doesn't improve the situation, you may have a bigger problem and should consider calling a plumber.

The Great Thaw

If you wake up to uncharacteristically cold weather one fine winter morning, you may find that all you can get out of your faucets are weird clunking sounds and no water. Standing water inside water pipes is a standing invitation to chill out if the temperature gets cold enough. In the worst cases, as ice forms inside them the pipes will expand and can eventually burst. If you don't want to wait until spring rolls around for them to thaw, you can hurry things along by supplying a little heat.

After you've figured out where the frozen section of pipe is located—it will be in an exposed, but uninsulated section of the house, like a crawl space—you can thaw it with a:

- Hair dryer
- Heat lamp
- Heating pad

QUICK n PAINLESS

You have to thaw the pipe gradually. The laziest way to do it is with a heating pad. Just wrap it around the pipe and forget about it for a while. You may have to move it as it melts the ice, but that's easier than having to be present for the entire thawing.

Don't use a torch! Insurance companies really don't care to pay for fire damages when arson is suspected.

In Seattle, we rarely have many really cold winter days. During one of our atypical cold spells, a lot of pipes froze. One resident solved his problem by crawling under his house with a propane torch to thaw the ice in his service line. His work was short-lived; the house caught fire! He didn't have to worry about frozen pipes after that!

Easier yet is to pay attention to weather reports. If the great freeze is on its way, open one or two of your faucets until you have just a trickle coming out. This will keep the water moving and prevent it from freezing. If you put a container under the taps, you can save the water for your house plants!

IF YOU'RE SO
INCLINED

Take a look at your pipe situation while the weather is still warm—like in the middle of summer. If you don't like what you see, attend to it while you can still do the work in your shorts.

Getting Time on Your Side

	The Old way	The Lazy Way
Continually overload an old fuse circuit instead of reconfiguring and adjusting the load	Get plenty of fuses	15 minutes
Plunge a drain at the first sign of trouble vs. waiting until your big dinner party, when it clogs up unexpectedly	Pizza anyone?	5 minutes
Wrap your exposed pipes with insulation when the weather is warm vs. thawing them when they freeze during the snowstorm of the century	Don't be in a hurry for running water	20 minutes
Mapping out your circuits yourself vs. having your friends give you a hand	If it's a big house, a couple of days	1 hour
Turning off the water to the washing machine and go on vacation vs. cleaning up the mess if a hose leaks	You know how water can travel?	2 minutes

Painless Painting and Woeless Wall Repairs

At their most basic, paint and other coatings have one important purpose: to protect the surfaces over which they are applied. Moisture, dirt, sunlight, baby food flung hither and yon by toddlers, and more can all eat away at unprotected surfaces. Paint acts as the bodyguard, taking the blows day after day until it's so punch drunk that it needs to be re-coated.

The secondary purpose of all these coatings is more artistic: They please us, they're comforting to look at, they reflect who we are. Your friends may not understand your glossy green walls and lemon yellow trim, but that's not your problem. Painting schemes can be simple or complicated, but simple is a lot easier.

ALL THE WORLD'S A CANVAS

In the old days, painting was simpler—and a lot more toxic. Lead-based oil paint was the rule and brushes were used on

QUICK **n**' PAINLESS

Even if you use latex paint, be sure to wear a pair of latex gloves, especially when you do a big job. They make hand clean-up quicker, and you'll avoid rashes from scrubbing off dried paint.

everything, including walls, ceilings, and whole exteriors. Painters did some of their own mixing of whiting and thinners. Oil paints were long-drying and difficult to apply. The wonderful world of chemistry, as well as the Environmental Protection Agency, has changed all of that.

Today, latex paint rules. Everything is done in latex, or can be, and you can forget about brushes. Painters arm themselves with airless sprayers and rollers and five gallon buckets of paint. Brushes are still used, of course, but only minimally on new construction.

Paint is available in different sheens, or degrees of gloss, including:

- Flat
- Satin
- Semi-gloss
- High gloss

Most living-area walls are done in flat latex to soften the glare from room lights and sunlight. Flat latex also hides flaws in the walls and ceilings—especially drywall seams—because it reflects so little light.

Satin is normally used in kitchens and bathrooms because it's easier to clean. Semi-gloss is most often used on woodwork for the same reason and to allow the moldings and trim to stand out from the walls. High gloss is most often used on boats, unless you have marine fantasies and want your house to look like a cabin cruiser.

Basically, the higher the gloss, the easier it is to clean because the paint forms a tougher film.

White Out

There's a very good reason why designers and architects of tract homes and housing developments choose some shade of white paint for all the walls and woodwork: It's less offensive than most other color choices; it's the vanilla ice cream of the color palette. Also, it's uniform, doesn't require any guesswork, and makes it easier to sell the house. As a buyer, you get a house that's easy to touch up, and one that has a certain illusion of size because the rooms aren't broken up by a lot of different colors. If you're buying a software-paid-for mega mansion, this probably isn't an issue, of course, but for many homes this illusion is important.

It's safe to say that just about all new residential painted walls are coated with latex paint. This is the standard for several reasons including:

- Ease of application
- Good coverage
- Non-toxicity
- Quick drying time

Over time—it may only take a day—you will start bruising your walls. A gym bag will leave a mark, or your dog will decide the dining room wall is a good rubbing post. The sooner you touch up these spots, the easier

YOU'LL THANK YOURSELF LATER

Go through the paint before you need it for touch-ups and pour some of each finish into smaller containers. Mark them with the date and location of where the paint was used. No more messing with five gallon buckets for those quick touch-ups!

they will blend in, and the less re-painting work for you. There's nothing to it. For simple wall upkeep in a new house, you will need:

- Touch-up paint
- Cotton swabs
- Foam paint brush

Painting contractors normally leave leftover paint in a new house for the owners' use. Be sure you're using the correct paint! If the painter didn't mark the containers, just read the labels: flat latex for the living area walls, satin for the bathrooms and kitchen.

Cotton swabs are perfect for small touch-up jobs, like painting over nail holes that you have filled with Spackle. Just a drop of paint and no one will ever see it. And no brush to wash!

Paint fades as it gets exposed to light. The advantage of touching up different shades of white is that the new paint doesn't appear to be a mismatch against the surrounding area when you're standing in front of the wall. Nevertheless, if you can touch up with a cotton swab, it will be the least noticeable.

For larger areas, like scuff marks from dragging your briefcase against the wall in that tight hallway squeeze between the garage and the kitchen, use a foam brush. Apply the paint at normal coverage over the area affected and then fan the edges of the paint outward into the surrounding wall, essentially thinning it out. This way, the difference between the new paint and the old is gradual and isn't as noticeable.

QUICK n PAINLESS

The easiest way to do minor touch-ups? Do it all at once! Take a walk through the house with your brush and jar of paint and dab and brush out every mark you see. Do this once a month and you're always caught up!

Take the Work Out of Woodwork

The latex revolution has done wonders for walls, but not always for woodwork and doors. There is an array of finishes available now for covering wood and not all of them are touch-up friendly.

For both speed and smooth results, most new finishes on wood are sprayed instead of brushed on and the results can be beautiful. Here we enter into the world of exotic, super-fast-drying finishes full of toxic solvents and other fun stuff that, realistically, can't be brushed out, even for a quick touch up. You have a few options including:

1. Respray with the same material.

2. Touch up with latex.

3. Touch up with oil.

4. Leave it alone.

Paint stores sell small, hand-held sprayers for touching up with fast-drying finishes. Aside from matching paint, you'll need whatever gene-altering solvent goes with it. Unless you have a big spot on a door staring you in the face, I'd say skip this approach.

Touching up these finishes with oil or latex instead of the same type of paint breaks a cardinal rule of painting: apply only like materials over each other. Oil will stick—it sticks to just about anything—but it will yellow eventually and will no longer match the original finish. Latex probably won't stick unless you sand and prime the area to be touched up. Who needs that? That's too much work for such small jobs.

You can do a woodwork touch-up if a standard latex finish was applied rather than the exotic stuff. It's like doing a wall touch-up with a slightly different twist.

Since most trim and woodwork is coated with a glossier finish than the surrounding walls, you can't touch up a small, individual spot and expect it not to stick out from the surrounding paint.

The solution? Paint a broader section, but just do the smallest area that makes sense. If you have a paneled door with a mark on one of the panels, paint the entire panel, but nothing more! Don't get carried away, you want this to be simple! An entirely repainted panel won't stick out as much as a touch-up in the middle of it where you removed your daughter's Spice Girls sticker!

Walla Walla

Like painting, wall construction and finishing has changed over the years. No more plaster and lath (thin, narrow strips of wood formed in a latticework as a backing for plaster) with apprentices learning their trade by mixing tons of plaster on the job and hauling it around for journeymen plasterers. Now, drywall in ready-made sheets is nailed and screwed right to the wall studs without requiring any underlying lath.

The typical drywall finish in new construction is textured rather than smooth. A smooth finish would mean the taping (the finish work done to hide the joints formed where two sections of drywall meet) would have to be really good. That's a lot of work, especially if the drywall isn't perfectly flat! Texture comes to the rescue, covering up some small sins and all in all producing a good-looking wall.

Texture is sprayed on the entire house at one time. How do you match that kind of finish if you ever have to repair it? It's as effortless as pushing a button! For most textured drywall repairs, you'll need:

- Spackle and putty knife
- A can of matching spray texture material
- Latex caulk
- Wet rag
- Paint and paint brush

If you've ever used a can of aerosol whipped cream, then you've got the skills necessary to re-spray small areas of your walls with new texture. I do recommend that you first do a test shot outside or in the garage. Aim the can into a box and spray. Then you'll know how fast it comes out. There's more than one style of texture, so if you aren't sure about the product, ask the paint store clerk. The usual repairs you'll need to do include:

- Small cracks at the seams
- Gouges

From time to time, the paper or fiberglass tape used to cover drywall seams can lift or tear. All it takes is some movement in the wall framing. Your house isn't coming apart at the seams! It's just going through some growing pains.

YOU'LL THANK YOURSELF LATER

Touch up your walls regularly and you'll avoid spending your time and money on re-painting. You'll also avoid having to face those smudges and stains until the next big paint job!

For splitting seams:

1. Cover the floor with plastic.

2. Lightly clean away any loose joint compound from the tape.

3. Press some latex caulk into crack and under the drywall tape.

4. Press the tape flat and wipe away excess caulk with your rag.

5. When the caulk has dried, spray it with texture according to the directions on the can.

6. Apply two coats of finish paint.

Relax, take your time, and you'll come out looking like a pro!

If you have a gouge, spackle the area and allow it to dry. Spray on the aerosol texture and paint when it has dried. For deep holes—1/2" or so—you'll need to apply two or three layers of Spackle, allowing each one to dry before applying the next. If you try to apply it all at once, it won't dry properly and will shrink and crack.

A House of Another Color

Older homes normally have some form of drywall as well. Plaster started dying out in the 1940s. Any building innovation that could cut the labor costs down always eventually got adopted by contractors, and drywall was no exception. These walls can be repaired and patched the same way as newer walls. The paint touch-up will depend on:

QUICK 📀 PAINLESS

You really want the easiest and laziest repair of all? Cover it up! A painting, wall hanging, or family photo can work wonders. This solution will make your home more colorful and interesting, and solve your wall problem at the same time.

- The age of the existing paint.
- The general condition of the paint.
- The likelihood of matching the paint.

Given enough time, and use, an interior wall may be an unlikely candidate for paint touch-up. Too much fading or the general grime of life and any touch-up you do might stick out worse than the offending marks! If you don't have any of the original paint to work with, you'll have to get it matched at a paint store, a sometimes "iffy" process (although the new computerized matching systems are usually pretty good).

At this point, it's best to leave it until you're ready to repaint. When you do repaint, keep it low key and manageable:

1. Break the job into small sections.

2. Decide how much time you want to work each day and stick to this schedule.

3. Do minimum clean up until the job is finished.

Small sections could mean one wall or one room. If you have a half an hour after work each night to do the job, you'll be finished with most rooms by the weekend. Don't sweat it; do enough each day to move the project along and then walk away from it (unless you really like painting).

There's no need to do a full clean up if you can just close the door to the room! Out of sight, easily out of mind.

IF YOU'RE SO
INCLINED

Wall painting goes faster with a big roller, so get the longest one available. Spend a few dollars more for a professional quality roller. Cheap ones won't hold as much paint, and will make the job take more time than necessary.

Brushes and rollers need to be kept clean, but they don't have to be 100-percent paint-free every time you're done using them. Just rinse them until most of the paint is out and, while they're still moderately damp, wrap them in plastic bags and seal them tightly. They'll easily last until the next day or so without drying out. Some people recommend putting them in the freezer, but I'm not a fan of that approach. Another alternative is to tightly wrap the brush in plastic wrap, then place it in a plastic bag, seal it, and put it in your refrigerator. Beware: if it isn't wrapped tightly, the paint fumes can be absorbed by some of the foods in the refrigerator. You could discover this when you butter your toast and it tastes like the Matador Red latex paint you used in your guest room!

Woodwork in older homes often has been repainted with oil or latex. If the house is old enough, the original paint on the woodwork may have been oil-based. If you need to repaint or touch up and you're not sure what kind of paint to use, chip a small piece of your existing paint from an out of the way piece of woodwork. Take this to an experienced paint store and they can set you up with the correct material for your job.

Mastering Plastering

The original walls in old homes are usually covered with plaster. They have an entirely different "feel" to them than drywall. Wet plaster was troweled over and pressed into lath, which acted as a framework to hold the plaster in place. Three different layers were applied, including the final finish coat. It was a ton of work and is rarely done today on new residential construction.

Patching plaster walls is a little more involved than patching drywall, but minor repairs are easy. Before you start, you should:

1. Take a good look at your walls and ceilings.

2. Evaluate the cracks: Do they really need repair?

3. Decide where to stop.

Some people see character in plaster cracks and some people see, well, cracks, and they don't like them. Repairing loads of small cracks can be very tedious. But there's an easy out if you have better ways to spend your time!

A coat of paint applied with a very coarse roller will cover a multitude of cosmetic problems painlessly. Normally, interior walls are painted with smooth rollers. But exterior stucco, for example, requires a coarser roller to hold more paint and to work it into the surface of the stucco. If you don't mind a less-than-smooth wall finish, this will do the trick inside, too, covering up many of those small, nuisance cracks, and maybe even some larger ones!

Otherwise, to do a quick plaster crack repair:

1 Lightly dig into the crack with a putty knife.

2 Apply a coat of Spackle.

3 When dry, sand the Spackle smooth.

4 Prime dried Spackle patches.

5 Paint.

Some cracks may return without more extensive repair, and new ones may emerge. In an old house, perfection is even more fleeting than in a new one. Don't complicate your life. Do the basic repairs, paint over everything with a coarse paint roller, and don't worry about it.

Get a Lead on Lead

Lead-based paint reigned supreme when old houses were built. It is likely that your woodwork, if it was originally painted rather than varnished, may have been coated with lead-based oil paint. In the years since, it could have been painted again with just about anything: oil, latex, or some more recent sprayed on application.

As long as you touch up the existing paint with the same type of paint, you'll be okay. If you're uncertain what it is, take a small sample of it to a paint store and inquire. This will be especially helpful if you're planning on a complete repainting.

Getting Time on Your Side

	The Old Way	The Lazy Way
Completely clean a brush after each use during a job vs. wiping it off	Gallons of water and minutes each time	2 minutes
Regular touch up vs. complete repainting	Hours!	Minutes
Patching a major hole and repainting vs. covering it with a picture	1 hour	5 minutes
Cleanup after spilling paint because you didn't think you needed a dropcloth vs. covering the floor with plastic	Hello, A-1 carpet sales?	Man, rolling up this plastic is killing me
Painting your front door with oil paint on a wet, fall day and having to close it vs. painting it on a happy, warm, summer day	Staying up all night to guard against intruders	Bedtime, I'd better lock up
Using cheap brushes vs. good ones	Loose bristles do this?	Wow, am I a good paint drier

fifteen

Simple Steps to a Firm Footing: Vinyl, Carpet, Tile, and Wood Flooring

Floors are kind of our ultimate household link to gravity. We walk on them, slide our furniture across them, break dishes against them and, in some households, ride Harley-Davidsons on them. Structurally, unless you've got an epidemic proportion of rot, a house that was accidentally built over a huge sinkhole, or some really aggressive and selective termites who favor floor joists, you never have to worry about your floors. Roofs may leak, windows break, and pipes burst, but you would be hard-pressed to find a case of a floor randomly collapsing.

In the nostalgic days of the last century, long before the days of weekend specials advertising three rooms of carpeting for $750 (including pad), wood floors were the norm. In more modest homes, good old Mom got stuck with cleaning them with a broom followed by hot water, lye, and a scrub brush.

QUICK ⬭ PAINLESS

Linoleum, which was introduced in the latter part of the 19th century, was a big improvement in terms of sanitation and maintenance.

Put Your Foot Down

Sheet vinyl and vinyl floor tiles are used today in most kitchens and bathrooms and are a better bet than linoleum. Wall-to-wall carpeting has replaced area rugs, and tile is used in entry ways, kitchens, and bathrooms, too. Wood floors will always be with us. Our parents couldn't wait to cover them up with carpet and say good-bye to dust balls and waxing. Their kids came along and bought houses as old or older than their parents', yanked the carpets up, and refinished the oak, fir, pine, and maple floors. In about 15 years from now, they'll start covering them with carpet again until their kids prove the inevitability of life repeating itself by rediscovering the wood floors when they become homeowners, and refinishing them one more time.

VOTE FOR VINYL

Let's face it, the most practical interior floor finish for families and pets is concrete covered with removable Astroturf, which can be removed, taken outside, and hosed off once a week. Okay, moving the furniture might be a problem, but conceptually this would work great until the kids are about 20 years old and go off to the big city.

Second choice would be vinyl—everywhere. It doesn't hold dust mites like carpet and it's a snap to clean. But we're human and not invariably practical. Comfort matters, so we use vinyl in those areas where sanitation is paramount: the kitchen and the bathrooms. About your only maintenance will be regular cleaning.

Vinyl floors have a few weak points, such as:

- Poor spot adhesion

- Tears and holes

- Blisters

Occasionally, and this is especially true at seams and edges, the adhesive isn't sufficient to hold vinyl tight. But repairs can be done pretty quickly. You will need:

- Vinyl adhesive or mastic

- Putty knife

- Rag

- Plastic wrap

- A heavy weight

1 Gently peel the loose edge up and scrape away any loose adhesive.

2 Apply new adhesive onto the underlayment and press the vinyl back down, pushing out any excess adhesive and wiping this up with your rag.

3 Place the plastic wrap over the repaired area (in case any more adhesive oozes out).

4 Place the weight over the plastic and leave it on for one full day.

IF YOU'RE SO
INCLINED

For extra life from your vinyl, protect it by putting hard plastic cup protectors under your furniture legs. These will prevent depressions and accidental tears.

This goes so quickly, you'll spend more time buying the materials than doing the work!

The vinyl society apparently has a rule that its members must always come loose and lift when laid up to and against the edge of a bathtub or shower. These seams are usually caulked as well as the others, but they never last. You can re-glue and re-caulk, or, do a one-time repair and screw a metal strip down over the edge of the vinyl and then forget about it. To do this, you will need:

- Tape measure
- Metal edge
- Hacksaw
- Hammer
- Caulk and caulk gun

Metal edges come in a variety of colors and styles. Check out what's available at a home builder's store or a flooring center. Cut it to size so it will run the entire length of your tub or shower stall.

1. After you've removed any loose caulking and applied new adhesive to the vinyl, press the metal strip firmly onto the floor and up to the edge of the tub. The strip will come with a package of nails with a matching finish. Hammer these through the pre-drilled holes in the metal.

2. After the strip is secured, apply a thin bead of caulk between it and the tub and at each of its ends. Do this once, and you'll probably never repair this vinyl again!

3. Tears and blisters are handled the same way you handle loose edges. With a blister, cut through the bubble with a sharp knife and then re-glue, weighting the area down for 24 hours.

What do you do about holes? Take the easy way out and place a throw rug over them. Unless you've got matching material, you won't be able to satisfactorily repair them anyway. A rug is a simple, quick fix and it always works. Besides, it just might help keep the floor cleaner, too!

Toxicity City

Some older vinyl and linoleum floors were manufactured with asbestos fibers. This isn't much of an issue for minor repairs, but it's a big deal if you decide to strip all the old material and replace it with new. You must follow asbestos abatement rules. If you pay to have it removed, it can be very expensive. Your local EPA office can send you down the river of no return in this matter.

WONDERFUL WALL-TO-WALL

Well, that's how is was originally sold anyway. Carpet was sold not only for its comfort, but for ease of maintenance. Hardwood floors were normally covered with large area rugs, but the borders still showed. Dust collected there, and the wood cried "wax me" every few months. Covering the whole floor with tightly stretched carpet solved this problem.

Regular carpet maintenance requires two items:

- A good vacuum cleaner
- A stereo headset

An upright vacuum cleaner with a beater bar is a better choice than a suction-only vacuum. The beater bar helps to loosen ground-in dirt, which is then pulled into

IF YOU'RE SO INCLINED

An easier solution? Cover all of your old floor with new plywood or particle board underlayment and install your new floor right over it. This will require some trimming around doors and some kind of beveled transitions between the new floor and the old adjacent floors.

the vacuum bag. What's the secret to good vacuuming (and a longer carpet life)? Do it slowly. That's where the headset comes in.

A slow, almost languid sweep with your vacuum will do a much better job than repeated, quick passes. Put on your favorite music and take your time. If you want to speed it up, buy the widest vacuum cleaner you can find. Check out janitorial supply stores for commercial models. Regular cleanings, at least once a week, will extend the life of your carpet. It's easier and cheaper than replacing it!

Rugs to the Rescue

Wear and tear on some areas of your carpet is unavoidable, even if you have a "no shoes" policy in your house. The very best carpet will hold up longer, but, eventually, everything wears down. Solution? Throw rugs. Cover up the spot and forget about it. Simple, easy, and inexpensive, what more could you want?

Same thing with deep-set stains. If they won't come out, and you're not ready for a professional cleaning, cover them. It doesn't get much simpler than that!

Fungal Bungle

As tempting as it may be, don't carpet your kitchen or bathrooms. Bathrooms are naturally wet and moist. The last thing you need is hostile colonization by strange microbes in your carpet which, before you can shampoo them out of existence, will go before the United Nations to demand free destiny. Better to put a machine-washable rug down over a vinyl or tile floor.

YOU'LL THANK YOURSELF LATER

Go to the best carpet store in town and get some of the cleaners that they recommend for removing stains, such as Host Emergency Pack. They also may have printed advisories for removing all types of spilled foods and liquids. Do this before you have a problem!

This is also true in the kitchen. Think of it this way: Would you rather clean up a piece of lemon meringue pie from a vinyl floor or out of a medium-pile carpet?

Shampoo, Rinse, and a Little Off the Top

Every grocery and hardware store in America seems to rent carpet shampooing equipment for do-it-yourselfers. Weekly coupons in your mail will bring you offers to shampoo and clean three rooms and a hallway for $29.95, followed by an asterisk indicating what's extra, like deodorizer and stain repellent. All these approaches do an adequate, but not terrific, job. There are two problems with them, one stemming from the other. They are:

1. The lack of power in the machinery.

2. The amount of water and soap left in the carpet.

The trick to cleaning carpet is to get the cleaning solution in and out of the carpet quickly and thoroughly. A low-powered machine will leave both soap residue and water in the carpet. The soap will attract new dirt and the water isn't exactly the best thing for the carpet pad. Aside from that, if it's too wet, microscopic wildlife can decide that your carpet is a cozy spot to put down roots.

Is this a huge problem? After all, people have been renting these machines for years or calling the DeLuxo Carpet Magicians to do the cleaning without any huge consumer backlash. Basically, it's a matter of getting what you pay for.

The laziest choice is to hire it out to professionals and have the work done while you're on vacation. If you just need a quick clean, hire the guys with the van and don't

IF YOU'RE SO
INCLINED

Take a lesson from some carpet professionals, who don't believe in mechanical carpet cleaning at all. They simply spot-clean on a regular basis with a dry, powdered carpet cleaner, and vacuum frequently. This is especially appropriate for more expensive carpets.

let them talk you into any of the extras. One easy way to cut down on your carpet cleaning is to use a large door mat. Keep the dirt outside, and your life inside will be a little simpler.

SMILE WITH TILE

Tile dates back to 4000 B.C. Egypt. You never know, some of the originals may still be hanging around a few public restrooms in Cairo. Back then, tiles were handmade, baked clay with hand-painted designs and glazes. Modern ceramic-glazed tiles have almost space-age qualities: They're not affected by oxygen so they don't fade, they can withstand high temperatures, and they're resistant to most acids, alkalies, and organic solvents. It's safe to say that they'll stand up to most household abuse.

Grout—the material that forms the seals between the tile pieces—is a little more pervious. Grout is porous and needs to be sealed periodically with a penetrating sealer. The sealer keeps water from seeping through the grout and helps prevent it from staining when any of the above acids, alkalies, or other fun stuff spills on it.

Other than that, tile requires very little maintenance. Regular cleaning with a mild household cleaner followed by a rinse with clear water and then a wipe dry, and you're done. The rinse is important so that a soap film doesn't form on the tile. You can tell if your floor isn't clean once you start slipping on it from built-up dirt, soap residue, and dampness.

QUICK n̲ PAINLESS

Professional cleaners, who charge appropriately, bring truck-mounted machines that really get things clean. Regardless of how you decide to clean your carpet, be sure it's dry before you start walking on it!

Your maintenance list for tile is short and sweet:

1. Wash and dry regularly.

2. Wipe up spills as they occur.

3. Apply a penetrating sealer to the grout according to sealer instructions and scheduling recommendations.

GOODY, THE FLOOR'S A WOODY

Wood floors remained the floor material of choice into the 1940s, mostly because there wasn't much choice. Wall-to-wall carpet is a post-World War II phenomenon. Before southern U.S. carpet factories started cranking up the looms, oak, fir, pine, and maple floors were hammered down from one end of the country to the other.

Standard wood flooring has since been supplemented with new, improved, fortified versions of hardwood, including pre-finished and acrylic-impregnated wood flooring. These are the simplest of all to take care of if you believe the manufacturers' claims of wax-free, no-care floors for life. All in all, they're pretty good, but apparently these guys never had a pair of Labrador Retrievers chase the house kitty from morning 'til night, all three sets of claws digging in along the way.

Clean as a Whistle

New wood floors are either the manufactured variety, that is, pre-finished, or they're raw wood, installed and finished on site. Pre-finished floors come with multiple coats of factory applied finish and are highly resistant to wear, spills, and fading. They need no maintenance other than:

QUICK 🔘 *PAINLESS*

Keep a spray bottle of mild household cleaner and water close by to quickly clean spills on tile. A few swift sprays and you won't be slipping away the next time you walk across your floor!

1. Vacuuming.

2. Regular mopping with approved cleaners.

3. Wiping up spills.

4. Using door mats when coming in from the outside.

Vacuuming should be done with a floor attachment, not with an upright vacuum cleaner's beater bar! These can catch small bits of debris, LEGO pieces, and Grape-Nuts, and drag them across the finish, leaving scratches.

If you want to go really low tech, the traditional cleaner on these and any other wood floor, is one cup of white vinegar mixed into a gallon of water. Unfortunately, this mix isn't such a great cleaner, but more of a rinse. Try Murphy Oil Soap or a cleaner recommended by a wood flooring supplier instead. Remember, when the manufacturer says "no wax," they mean no wax! Why make work for yourself? Wax will just build up and make future cleanings a nuisance. Keep it simple, as always, and just mop with a small amount of cleaner and water.

That's it, just figure it into your housecleaning and you're done!

Floors that are installed and finished on site will not be as resistant as pre-finished floors to the rough-and-tumble life that goes on upon them. Typically, these floors are finished with:

- A urethane floor finish

- Swedish finish

- Penetrating sealer

Wooden floors in kitchens—and even bathrooms—are trendy in newer houses, but they're not such a great idea in these rooms. If you have them, cover up the heavy traffic areas with washable rugs to protect the floors.

The Lazy Way

Urethanes and Swedish finishes are tough film-forming materials that seal and protect the wood. Usually two to three coats are applied. There are also water-based clear finishes that are environmentally friendly, but endurance challenged.

Penetrating sealers soak into the wood and form a slight waxy film on its surface. These are the least resistant finishes and need regular buffing and reapplication. Some people prefer the appearance of these finishes, and that's why they choose them. This will probably work if you never have children, animals, guests, or shoes in your house. Otherwise, stick with a tougher finish.

Ooh, What Character!

That's usually what's said about everything in old houses, and it's true, but, as in any decent fiction, you're hoping some characters will find redemption. Old homes in many parts of the country most often had oak or fir floors. Colonial period homes and those in the Southeast often sported pine floors, which gives you insight into what Scarlett O'Hara really meant when she said she was pining away for Ashley.

If you're one of the owners-down-the-road of a house built some years ago, your wood floors may well have been refinished at least once. The refinishing process typically involves sanding all of the old varnish off—and a 1/16" of an inch or so of the wood—and applying new floor finish. This is a smelly, noisy, messy job, and well worth having someone else carry it out. Before you decide to refinish your floors, consider:

IF YOU'RE SO
INCLINED

Maintain urethane and Swedish finished floors the same way as pre-finished floors, but consider some throw rugs for heavy traffic areas. Throw rugs are uncomplicated and labor-free. Buy the rugs, and keep your relationship with your floors on the right footing.

1. Can they be buffed and waxed instead?

2. Is there enough wood left to sand safely?

3. What about carpet?

It's much less complicated (and cheaper) to buff your floors with a floor cleaner and then wax than to sand and refinish. They won't look like new, but they may be vastly improved. Ask yourself if your lifestyle will really support refinished floors. Do you have active kids? Pets? Friends who use your living room for impromptu rugby games? Test an out-of-the-way spot with:

- Fine steel wool and rags
- Floor cleaner/restorer
- Wax

Clean one square foot of your floor with steel wool and a floor cleaner from a rental shop. Buff in some wax. Is this acceptable? Can you live with the results? If so:

1 Rent a floor buffer with steel wool pads and a polishing pad.

2 Thoroughly clean the floor.

3 Buff in the wax.

This won't remove deep scratches, but it should buff out a lot of the superficial ones. Take one day during a weekend—depending on the size of your floor—to buff it up and think about the money you saved by putting off the refinishing!

Wood floors can usually take up to three sandings before they say, "Forget it, there isn't enough of me left to sand." A professional floor refinisher can tell you if your floors have had it or whether they can go one more round. If they can't, ask the contractor about alternative refinishing methods or installing new wood floors.

If none of that appeals to you, consider carpet. It may not be as quaint as wood, but it covers up a lot of problems and is comfortable to walk upon. It's an easy out!

Before installing carpet, check that:

1. There are no missing pieces of flooring.

2. You have secured any loose flooring.

3. You have eliminated as many squeaks as possible.

Missing flooring can be patched in with anything that's the same dimension, even plaster patching compounds. Loose flooring can be nailed or screwed to the sub-flooring.

Sneak Up on Squeaks

Wood is absorbent. Even after it's kiln-dried, it can still absorb some moisture, especially in humid climates. Like any wood, when it gets wet, it expands; when it dries out, it shrinks. Movement in floor boards won't be major by any means unless they get flooded and the water stays around too long.

So where do those squeaks come from? They occur when the edge of one floorboard rubs up against an adjoining board because one or both of them has slightly expanded. The cure? Talcum powder! Sprinkle it

YOU'LL THANK YOURSELF LATER

Walk over your entire floor and mark any squeaks or loose boards with chalk or masking tape. Repair all of them before the happy carpet installers show up, because it isn't their job to do any floor repairs.

liberally between the offending floor boards, and the squeaks should be greatly reduced. The powder absorbs the moisture and acts as a slight buffer between the boards. Push the powder in with a duster or dust mop and lightly vacuum the excess.

Getting Time on Your Side

	The Old Way	The Lazy Way
Refinishing vs. buffing the downstairs floors	Before or after repairing the gouges?	2 hours
Refinishing the downstairs floors vs. buying some area rugs	Could I have been a little too aggressive with the sander?	Write a check for the rugs
Refinishing the downstairs floors vs. hiring it out	I hadn't believed those warnings on the paint cans	Yes, we'll do your floors while you're on vacation
Installing white carpet vs. a neutral color when you have two kids and a Labrador puppy	Rent a carpet shampooer every month	I know I spilled a bag of soil around here somewhere
Installing a big door mat and removing your shoes in the house vs. lumbering around with your work boots on	Good thing we have a 24-hour vacuum system	Vacuum cleaner? Didn't we loan it to Frank a couple of years ago?
Ignoring the grout in your bathroom vs. sealing it regularly	I happen to like the color of mildew	Yes, my grout won me the Most Improved Camper Award

Go with the Air Flow: Keep Your Furnace Burning and Your Air Conditioning Cool

If you long for the simpler days of gathering around the family fireplace for heat and comfort, let me suggest that you start buying a lot of sweaters and leggings. Once you step about two feet away from the fire, like our ancestors, you'll freeze, regardless of how much wood you cut. Actually, cutting the wood will probably keep you warmer than burning it in the fireplace. Modern heating systems have shrunk to the point that a furnace that used to be the size of a Volkswagen is now the size of a steamer trunk. And they work better than ever.

Air conditioning has given us the opportunity to live in climates hitherto suited only to lizards and cacti, as well as allowed the establishment of the world's biggest gambling

Many old furnaces have asbestos-wrapped ducts. Old hot water boilers may be wrapped in it as well. Asbestos removal is expensive and will increase the cost of replacing your furnace, so be prepared.

operations in the middle of desert nuclear wasteland. Like any other machinery with moving parts, heating and cooling systems need some looking after and regular check-ups. Spend a little time each month doing this and you'll never lose your cool.

Hot and Cool (Temperatures, Not Personality Traits)

The main residential heating systems are:

1. Forced air natural gas

2. Oil furnaces

3. Hot water or steam heat

4. Electric furnaces and baseboard heating

If your house is old enough to have its original "octopus" furnace (so-called because of its massive, tentacle-like system of ducts) it may have originally been a coal furnace later converted to oil. Often, these furnaces would later be converted one more time to natural gas. The operation of a gas furnace is pretty simple.

Natural gas is piped into the house and its volume is recorded by your gas meter. The gas is burned inside a heat exchanger. Once the heat exchanger has heated, a blower pulls cold air from the house through a cold-air return, or intake, that moves it over the heat exchanger, where it is heated and circulated throughout your house.

Your thermostat controls the temperature of your house. Well, realistically, the interplay of complex family dynamics ("I'm cold." "Leave the thermostat alone." "It's too hot in here!") controls the temperature, but your thermostat tries its best to accommodate all comers. If you really want to control the heat, install two thermostats: hide one, and leave the other out in the open, but unconnected to the furnace. It will be years before anyone figures out that you've been messing with them, and by that time they'll have gotten used to the idea of layering their clothing. The exhaust gases are vented out of the house, either through a chimney or a wall vent. Modern, high-efficiency furnaces no longer require chimneys for venting.

What do you need to do? Not much:

1. Have it serviced once a year.

2. Clean or replace the filter every four to six weeks during heating season.

3. Oil any motors requiring regular lubrication.

4. Know where your gas shutoff valve is located.

5. Check the ducts in the crawl space for proper fastening.

6. Have your duct work cleaned every five years.

Beat the Freeze

The idea of yearly maintenance for a furnace that seems to be running just fine is very parental (not that they ever did it), very boring, and not done nearly enough. Human beings prefer drama to predictability. Thus, having the furnace die in the middle of the worst freeze of the century is much more sensational than saying you

IF YOU'RE SO
INCLINED

It's far lazier (read easier) to call your heating repair service in late summer and have your furnace checked than to wait until January, when finding an available service person is about as likely as finding someone in Seattle who doesn't drink coffee.

YOU'LL THANK YOURSELF LATER

Buy a box of replaceable filters and keep them near the furnace. That way you can have a season's supply ready to go without having to run out to the store every month. It's one less thing to think about and less expensive, too!

avoided it by having your furnace serviced in August. It's not the kind of story that you'll get to embellish over the years, either, but what's more satisfying than watching bowl games without having to watch your breath vaporize? Besides, you can always make up furnace-related horror stories; just be sure none of the original witnesses are within earshot.

Yearly service will include a filter change or cleaning and a system check. You should also ask the technician to check for CO (carbon monoxide) leaks. Carbon monoxide results from incomplete combustion of the gas. It really does a number on your hemoglobin, and is reason enough to have your furnace inspected and serviced yearly. It's money well spent, and all you have to do is pick up the phone! If you happen to be a visiting alien whose hemoglobin needs a daily carbon monoxide fix, let your furnace technician know this during the servicing.

Most furnaces have easily replaceable filters. Some have reusable filters that can be cleaned and reinstalled. Clean or change your filter monthly during the heating season and keep your furnace running efficiently with less effort. This is usually a five-minute, nothing-to-it job. Do it at the same time you take out your trash—pull the filter out, toss it in the trash, and install its replacement. There's a new generation of allergen-catching replaceable filters that you may want to try. They're about twice the price, but work very well. Clean filters are especially important if you've got shedding dogs or cats in the house—or humans for that matter. Whichever you use, the job is done for another month!

There is at least one circumstance in which changing the filter isn't very easy. Downflow furnaces (furnaces with duct work attached at the top of the furnace to pull the air down) can have barely accessible filters, depending on how they were fitted during installation. Ask your service technician about installing access panels for easier filter removal. Then, write to the furnace manufacturer and tell them what you think of their thoughtlessness for not installing the filters in an accessible place.

In older furnaces, the motors sometimes need to be oiled. If your only experience with oil is the olive oil variety, when you have your yearly service done, have the service technician show you what to do. A couple of squirts of SAE-20 weight oil and two quick minutes of your time and your motor will be humming along!

Something Smells Funny

Natural gas can be toxic, but has no odor. What you smell is a chemical odorant added to the gas so you can detect a leak by smelling it. If this happens, don't light a trendy cigar before you:

1. Get your kids and pets out of the house.

2. Shut off the gas.

3. Open windows and doors.

4. Call the gas company.

5. Put on a sweater and open your windows and doors, too, if needed.

The gas company takes gas leaks very seriously so call them immediately.

IF YOU'RE SO INCLINED

While you're familiarizing yourself with your gas shutoff, check any individual gas appliances for the pilot light instructions. They go out occasionally, and have to be relit.

Take the time to locate your gas shutoff valve, preferably before you have a potential emergency. If it requires a special tool, such as a wrench, to turn off the gas, keep it nearby and visible. Also, take a few minutes to show all the adults in your house how to shut off the gas. Test the valve by turning it partway (if you shut it all the way off, you'll have to go around and light all your pilot lights again).

When Ducts Run Amok

Do you have a furnace that runs and runs, but your living room is still so cold that NASA uses it to test new space suit designs? Check the heat register. Sometimes the duct work running through the crawl space comes loose—especially if the installer didn't use enough straps—and pulls away from the register. The result is that all the heat is pumped out down below by the furnace instead of into the room. This is great for certain subterranean life forms under your house who'll think they won a trip to Bermuda.

Re-attaching loose, flexible ducts is a quick job. You will need:

- Straps
- Hammer and nails

Go to your hardware store or home improvement center and tell a clerk what you're trying to do. Either metal or plastic straps will do the job. Wherever it looks like the duct could use a lift, wrap it with a strap and nail the strap to the joist overhead. You'll need only a few for each run of duct work. Do this once, and secure the ends

Congratulations! You've emerged victorious from the catacombs under your house, and now everyone's warm again. Kick the NASA guys out of your living room and sit back with the morning paper and a cup of coffee.

The Lazy Way

of any loose ducts to their registers and you should never have to go down there again!

If your duct work is in an uninsulated area it will save energy, and work more efficiently.

Bust That Dust!

If you're religious about changing your filters, your duct work will remain pretty clean. Even so, talk with your furnace technician about recommendations for cleaning them. Ducts collect dust, pet hair, and small toys the same way the areas behind refrigerators do because they're there. Get a recommended service to come and vacuum yours out.

If yours is a newly built house, cleaning the construction dust out of the ducts is a good idea. Otherwise, ducts need cleaning only every five to 10 years, depending on the dust level in your local environment.

Striking Oil

Oil heat used to be top gun before natural gas started to strut its stuff. Oil has some advantages: It offers the consumer a choice of competitive suppliers, it's a stable and safe fuel, and it has low carbon monoxide content compared to gas. But gas is continuously supplied and you don't have to depend on truck deliveries.

What's the easiest way to take care of your oil furnace? Have it serviced once a year. Have the technician point out the unit's lubrication requirements and show you how to accomplish them. There, a done deal. A short lecture by a technician and some easy follow up by you and you'll be warm all winter long!

QUICK ⬤ PAINLESS

Just make the call and schedule an inspection. Ask the technician for any tips or pointers that may help your system run more efficiently throughout the year. If it's needed, the technician will also bleed any air from the system so your radiators will heat properly.

You're in Hot Water Now

Hot water and steam heat systems are great. This is a world of circulators, expansion tanks, cut-off switches, radiators, and evenly distributed warmth. It's also a world best left to technicians you should hire to inspect your system once a year. This is especially true since the system sits idle for many months out of the year.

Warm Currents—Electric Heat

Unless you're living right next to a major dam and have a direct tap to its generators, electric heat can be expensive. In new construction, electric baseboard or similar zone heating is sometimes installed because it's cheaper than installing a furnace with all of its accompanying duct work.

Individual room heaters are usually of a blower or radiant type, in which a series of metal fins direct the heat into the room. These heaters are generally reliable and only require an occasional vacuuming to keep them clear of dust and debris. The next time you're vacuuming the carpet, slip the upholstery attachment on and go over the heaters. Your maintenance is done without any extra work!

Electric furnaces need their filters changed regularly. If you have any electrical problems with either the furnace or the room heaters, call a technician! They don't call electricians "Sparky" for nothing, so let them handle your electrical problems.

YOU'LL THANK YOURSELF LATER

Most furnace maintenance, aside from replacing filters, is a once-a-year event. Since a yearly servicing is a good idea anyway, leave the maintenance to the technician.

Furnace First Aid

Sometimes, despite servicing, your furnace may quit. Maybe you offended it in a past life or maybe a fuse burned out. Motors are made of moving parts, just as we are, and eventually they give out. Sometimes they do it with warning (those strange new noises that you might mistake for mating calls with the water heater) and sometimes they just give up the ghost. Your problem may not be that drastic. A little bit of quick troubleshooting can save you a repair bill. If your furnace stops:

1. Turn the thermostat up above the room temperature.

2. Check your fuses or circuit breakers.

3. In older furnaces, check that the pilot light is still lit.

4. In modern furnaces, turn the thermostat all the way down for two minutes and then turn it up again to reset the ignition cycle.

5. For oil furnaces, check to be sure the emergency or service switch has not been accidentally turned off.

If none of the above work, call your service technician and relax. You'll have heat again, although at the price of a service call. It may be that you need a part replaced that could not be anticipated during the yearly service. Furnaces are like any other machines: Wear and tear take their toll. It's better than huddling around a fireplace!

A COMPLETE WASTE OF TIME

The 3 Worst Things to Do with Your Furnace

1. Ignore warning signs— like new, weird noises.

2. Skip regular maintenance.

3. Treat the filters as permanently installed components.

QUICK **n** PAINLESS

Cold Comfort

Air conditioning is another one of those once-a-year service check systems (those of you living in the Yukon can probably skip this section). Air conditioning is a closed system of copper tubing, a compressor, heat exchangers or coils, and more of the ubiquitous electronics that enter into just about every mechanical device we use. In addition to cooling us, air conditioning removes humidity, which really increases our comfort.

During a yearly servicing, a technician will:

1. Clean debris from the condenser.

2. Clean or replace filters.

3. Check the drive belt.

4. Inspect and lubricate the fan.

5. Check that the coil is clean and the system is properly charged.

As the owner, you should clean or replace the filters monthly and keep debris and plant life away from the outdoor condenser. If the unit maintenance calls for it, oil the fan every month with SAE-20 weight oil or another recommended lubricant. When you vacuum the floors, vacuum the grills and registers to keep dust and pet hair off them.

That's it: a quick shot of oil, a filter cleaning once a month, and a light vacuuming and you're a cool customer for the summer.

Getting Sense on Your Side

The Crazy Way	The Lazy Way
Treat your outdoor air conditioner condenser like a piece of sculpture: Hey, this heats up the place better than the furnace	Keep it clear of leaves and debris: Great, my nose is turning blue!
Constantly readjust the thermostat: Get all your exercise putting your sweater on and off	Keep the settings fixed to maintain a true comfort level: Does anyone know where the thermostat is?
Ignore the filter: Does the air seem a little thick in here?	Clean or change it it regularly: The lab test says my air is 99 percent pure
Ignore regular maintenance: Oh, well, spring comes early around here	Have a service technician check your furnace on a regular schedule: Send a fruit basket for the holidays
Never check your duct work: Is the furnace supposed to heat the living room?	Inspect loose connections: The underside of the house is so interesting; wish it had taken longer
Fix that hot water leak with duct tape: Hey, it's only a small puddle	Call a technician: Boy, was that phonecall exhausting

Loose Ends and Other Lazy Stuff

Look around your house hard enough—or even not very hard—and you can find something to clean or fuss with. If you attended to every stain, scratch, and squeaky hinge, you might well spend all of your spare time turning your home into a museum—a perfect time capsule of you. But even museums get dusty and the paint gets chipped off of a door here and there. Accept some imperfections—you'll have no choice in the matter if you have kids or dogs—and you can feel good about your home and have a life, too.

This chapter shows you ways to make being a responsible homeowner a little easier, so you can get rid of those museum docents who've been hanging around on call! To quote William James, another handy quotable guy for authors, "The art of being wise is the art of knowing what to overlook."

Get a Life!

Don't take James too literally. He didn't mean overlooking everything—although that may be tempting. Move into a motel and you can pull that one off, but your house has some work that can't be overlooked. Just take care of it the easy way and give yourself some more free time to read more James—or maybe something just a bit more contemporary. You can learn to do any and all repairs on your house. You can also learn to tune your car, build a solar-powered sewing machine from scrap parts, and make homemade cheese. Unless you value antisocial, survivalist behavior, do you really want to do all this? It's not like we're living in early 19th century America as self-sufficient farmers. We're urban kids, used to washing machines, espresso makers, and ATMs.

Even in the 19th century they grabbed every advance they could, from harvesters to better stoves. You ever try to cook a three course meal of mush, beans, and cornbread in the fireplace? Laziness—the ability to do regular chores more easily and efficiently—is part of our national heritage. Throw open your bedroom window and tell the world that you're lazy and proud of it. Then, take a look around at those nagging jobs, and come up with a plan.

Run for the Yellow Pages

When it comes to your house, there are definitely some tasks worth avoiding, unless you're highly motivated to do them. They include:

- Wallpapering
- Refinishing wood floors
- Installing vinyl or tile floors

YOU'LL THANK YOURSELF LATER

Talk with people who have done their own major work on their homes. Look at the results. See if their marriages survived; some don't! This will help you decide if the job is worth doing yourself.

Wallpapering seems very civilized until you realize it's 3 a.m., the pattern isn't matching very well, you're out of material, and the job isn't near finished.

Sanding and refinishing wood floors is a dusty, smelly mess.

The fun of running big sanders dissolves instantly when you realize how much work is involved. That floor had better be perfectly clean, or you'll be looking at that cat hair that's eternally encased in urethane forever.

You had better cut that vinyl just right or figure out some way to disguise your mishap.

Tile? Even experienced installers can find some jobs frustrating. You may discover a direct line to the family insanity you thought had died out with your great-great uncle Herman.

Choose your battles. Sometimes the easiest way to go is to find a new idea or find a contractor.

The Best Cure is Prevention

Avoiding problems is the easy way to maintain a home. Taking kind of a parental attitude, not as if any of our parents were the perfect, organized homeowners, makes for a more hassle-free home life.

Some problems can be avoided by:

1. Resealing bathroom and kitchen tile grout every two years.

2. Vacuuming refrigerator coils.

IF YOU'RE SO
INCLINED

If you're motivated to perform tasks others wouldn't and want to stay that way, do yourself a favor and read the chapters on The Lazy Way to get them done.

3. Caulking bathtub walls, and seams between tub and tile (after scraping and cleaning thoroughly with a bleach-based cleanser).

4. Vacuuming bathroom fan grilles.

There are other avoidance strategies throughout this book. Use them. They are hands down easier than dealing with bigger problems!

Tools Rule!

Evolution took a marvelous turn when it endowed us with opposable thumbs. Good thing, too, otherwise our pets might be feeding us dried pellets made from ingredients no one discusses publicly. Here are a few additional tool thoughts:

- A six-foot step ladder is a good size to have around the house.

- Work gloves will help prevent blisters from repetitive hammering, raking, or shoveling.

- Wrapping shovel and rake handles with foam pipe insulation will make them more comfortable to use.

- Keep all your power tool manuals and warranties in one file-along with appliance, TV, and stereo papers, as well.

- Mark your tools with an engraver so you can ID them later, like when your sister-in-law borrows them.

- Keep your extension cords neatly rolled up when not in use; if they're really a mess, hang them out of a second-story window and twist away the tangles.

- Hang your brooms up so the bristles don't get bent.

- Use a knee pad, available from a garden center, and your knees will thank you.

- Last, keep your tools orderly, and also keep them clean and oiled or sharpened for the next use. You'll find them quicker and get the job done faster—the best of both worlds!

Small-Job Secrets

Some ways of working are self-evident and some have to be discovered. That's why there are grandfatherly types around. You have to sort through the information since some of the materials they may recommend have been outlawed for years by the EPA. There's a certain inter-generational comfort from sitting around the old porch swing hearing stories about toxic finishes, used without the benefit of gloves or respirators, that, by golly, worked just great! Other advice is more useful, such as:

1. If a screw is too tight to remove, first try tightening it slightly; often, this will allow you to back it out.

2. Before climbing up an extension ladder, pound a couple of stakes in front of the legs to prevent it from slipping. Once you've climbed up, remember to tie the top of the ladder to the structure you've leaned it against.

3. To pour a small amount of liquid out of a gallon container, just slightly loosen the cap and let it dribble out; this way, it won't gush out and spill.

YOU'LL THANK YOURSELF LATER

Aluminum stepladders are lighter than wooden ones, but they like to conduct electricity at the worst times—which are at all times. Stay on the safe side and use wood.

4. An old beater from a kitchen mixer makes a great paint mixer; just attach it to your electric drill. If you want to be really cheap and easy about it, cut off a straight section of a wire clothes hanger, bend one end into a hook, and insert the other end into your drill. Keep it for reuse or toss it in the trash when you're finished.

5. Wipe the lids and rims of paint cans before sealing them up; this avoids the build-up of dried paint gunk and forms a better seal. Be sure the top of the can is marked with a date and the room for which its color was used. The date will let you know if it's way too old to use again.

6. If you have trouble holding small nails you need to hammer, put them between the teeth of a comb; now you have a quick nail holder and your fingers are out of the way.

Better Safe Than Sorry

Power tools are usually loud and fast moving. Let your mind wander for a few seconds and you can have big problems. They assault our ears with noise and our eyes with dust. Solvents hit the old olfactory system and aren't any fun at all. Some simple countermeasures are:

1. Keep several pairs of disposable ear plugs around at all times, even when vacuuming your house.

2. Use solvents only in well-ventilated areas.

3. Wear eye protection when appropriate.

YOU'LL THANK YOURSELF LATER

Buy eye protection that is comfortable. If the goggles or glasses fall off easily, hurt your head or neck, or have scratched or blurred lenses, you may actually cause more harm than good. And chances are, you won't choose to wear them often either.

4. Keep a first aid kit or two around your house and workshop.

5. Store all flammable finishes and solvents away from water heaters, furnaces, and children.

6. Pour all small amounts of used or old solvent in one can; when full, dispose of according to local regulations.

7. Keep fire extinguishers available in your kitchen, workshop, and garage.

It's a Cover-up, I Tell You

Disguise is a valuable art form. Where would we be without blond wigs, Groucho Marx mustaches, and fake noses when we need them? Unsightly, but not critical, damage or stains around a house are easily covered up. For example:

A large damaged section of a wall can be covered over with a tapestry or hanging decorative rug.

Stains, water damage, or cracks in a wood floor can be covered over with an area rug.

A heat-proof tile or piece of marble can be glued over a burned or otherwise damaged section of a kitchen countertop.

You'd be surprised how easily you can live with a huge bulge in your plaster after you've covered it up with a garage sale Oriental rug. Out of sight, out of mind, and outstandingly simple!

Painting parties—inducing your friends to help you paint by bribing them with meals and beer—work best for exterior painting. Warm up the barbecue and have some fun on the job.

The Lazy Way

YOU'LL THANK YOURSELF LATER

If your project is going to take several hours, prepare snacks and a meal ahead of time. This is the easy way to keep yourself fed and motivated. If you go out to lunch, you may not come back!

Take Some of the Pain Out of Painting

Painting can be very gratifying. The results—and the mess—are immediate. An otherwise grim-looking room can become the cheeriest part of the house. A few painless reminders include:

1. If the job requires several gallons of paint, empty each can into a single five-gallon bucket in order to box, or mix, them together. This ensures that the color will be uniform.

2. Decide if it's cheaper for you to buy an extra roller cover rather than clean the one you use for the job; roller covers hold a lot of paint and can be a nuisance to clean.

3. After cutting off the tip of a tube of caulk, stuff a long galvanized nail into the opening of the tube to prevent the caulk from drying out.

4. Some finishes (varnish, polyurethane, shellac, and others) should not be shaken or vigorously stirred; read all labels or ask the paint store clerk if you're uncertain.

5. Spray paint is good for very specialized uses, which don't include wall touch-ups. Read the label, and use it for appropriate surfaces onl—that means no graffiti!

Squawking About Squeaks

Hinges, floors, and mice all squeak. The first two are a little easier to attend to since they can't run away. For the non-rodent type of squeaks and other sticky situations, you can:

1. Spray WD-40 or silicone on hinges.

2. Use powdered graphite on door locks.

3. Sprinkle talcum powder or powdered graphite between squeaky floor boards.

4. If you have ceiling access under the floor, fill any gaps between the subflooring and the joist with small wood shims.

5. Nail wood braces between any loose joists.

6. Rub a sticking door with paraffin; if necessary, lightly sand first, touch up the paint, and then apply paraffin (also works for casement windows).

7. If necessary, you can nail through carpet; hammer a finishing nail flush to the floor. (There are great new screws that come with special jigs that allow you to break off the screw head after you've screwed it into the joist or subfloor).

8. Mice? Call an exterminator. Cats do a good job too, but tend to offer the remains to their owners as gifts.

Fire and Water

Well, we hope there's no fire. A few tips to remember:

1. Always turn the power off to any circuit you're working on.

2. Before you call an electrician or appliance technician, check that the power is on; you may have simply tripped a breaker or blown a fuse.

QUICK (n) PAINLESS

Does caulking your tub seem like a challenge? Simplify it. After you've cleaned out the old caulking and let the seam dry, line each side with masking tape! Apply silicone bathroom caulk, smooth it, and carefully remove the tape. Your results will look great!

3. Periodically pour some water down the drains of any unused tubs or sinks; this keeps the traps full of water so they block sewer gas from coming into your house.

4. If your glass shower doors are looking scummy, clean them with a sponge and white vinegar.

5. Fiberglass tub enclosures will regain some of their gloss with liquid auto wax.

6. Clean your aerators (these are found at the ends of faucets and allow water to come out evenly) by soaking them in vinegar once in a while; you can do the same for shower heads if they seem clogged.

Aerators and shower heads can be cleaned easily without removing them, too. Just partially fill a small plastic bag with vinegar and secure it around the end of the faucet or shower head. Let it sit overnight and it should dissolve some of the mineral build-up.

And the Government Gets the Last Word

The government has all kinds of free and inexpensive consumer-oriented material available by writing to:

Consumer Information Catalog

General Service Administration

P.O. Box 100

Pueblo, CO 81002

You may as well see what the government printing presses are cranking out for your benefit. Order enough of these catalogs and they may get too busy to print up your tax forms!

YOU'LL THANK YOURSELF LATER

A generally good idea is to photograph your house, inside and out. This will provide an inventory of your possessions and verify the condition of the house for insurance purposes. Keep these photos and a written description of the contents of your house in a safety deposit box.

Getting Time on Your Side

	The Old Way	The Lazy Way
Maintaining the perfect house to go with your perfect life vs. being realistic and forgetting about staying trim forever	Ashes to ashes, dust to dust	I had a great time.
Painting your three-story, six-color Victorian yourself vs. hiring the Gay Nineties Paint Company	Just 3 more weeks and I'll be done with the trim	Hey, I told you lemon-yellow on the rafters
Drilling away while you play with your dog vs. putting Rover out while you put up your bookshelves	So the hole's a little big; that's what big screws are for	Ah, just the right size, and in no time
Running a whining electric saw without ear plugs vs. plugging them in before you plug in your tools	Huh? What did you say?	Did I hear a yellow-bellied sapsucker?
Pulling apart a damaged electrical outlet with the power on vs. turning it off first	Hmm, another way to barbecue	Safe and sane wins again. Order in some barbecue

eighteen

Simple Scheduling Saves Snooze Time

Americans live by the clock. Morning alarms, meetings, day care hours, noon workouts—the last thing we want to do is schedule our free time, especially if it involves home maintenance! But by putting it off we almost guarantee that eventually we'll have to spend even more time at it! If your grandparents aren't in the room, it's okay to admit that all that advice about stitches in time saving nine and not putting off until tomorrow what you can do today had an element of truth in it (even if you thought it made them as boring as yesterday's software).

HOW DOES THURSDAY AT 3 A.M. LOOK?

Put on some classical music and sit down with a notepad and pen or your handy laptop PC. Your maintenance lists will have several components:

- Time of year
- Tasks
- Materials needed

We use schedulers and calendars for everything else in our lives, why not keep one for your house and keep on top of your maintenance the easy way? Bring those planning and management skills home, and you really will have more free time.

A list that follows the calendar is probably the easiest one to write. Some chores need to be done monthly, some only once a year. You'll have some maintenance to do to prepare for the seasons, and some as a result of seasonal wear and tear. There will always be something to do, but a list and schedule will help you keep your work-time to a minimum and your worry-time at zero.

Where do you start? How about New Year's Day?

Happy New Year! Now Get to Work

Well, I wouldn't recommend making up your schedule on New Year's Day unless you're Amish and your idea of a fun New Year's Eve is having an extra glass of apple cider. The first three months of the year might look something like this:

January

- Clean furnace filter.
- Check gutters for ice build-up (indicates they may not be draining).
- Vacuum furnace registers in rooms.
- Oil any furnace motors as required.
- Lubricate garage door tracks and rollers, tighten screws or fasteners.
- Clean drains monthly with baking soda/vinegar mix; pour boiling water down kitchen sink and tub drains once a week.
- Remind yourself where the water, gas, and power shutoffs are located.

- Touch up interior wall paint as needed.
- Spot-clean carpet in heavy traffic areas with dry powder carpet cleaner.
- Check GFI outlets and breakers.
- Vacuum the coils both behind and under your refrigerator (every three to four months).
- Wash your reusable filters from your range hood over your stove and replace any charcoal filters.
- Partially drain hot water heater to remove sediment (every six months).
- Check all smoke detectors.

Uh, oh. You're thinking, if I do everything on this list I won't have time for any of my New Year's resolutions like learning to play classical banjo or taking up conversational Sanskrit. Okay, let's see how long this will really take.

- Furnace filter: five to 10 minutes
- Check gutters: five minutes
- Vacuum heat registers: five minutes
- Oil motor: five minutes
- Lubricate garage door tracks: five minutes
- Clean drains: 10 minutes
- Pour boiling water in drains: how long does it take for the water to boil? Add two minutes per drain for travel time.
- Shutoff reminder: two minutes
- Paint touch-up: 15 minutes

Make up your schedule and then take days off for your birthday, Hungarian Independence Day, Groundhog Day— you're the boss—you can declare your own holidays!

The Lazy Way

QUICK ⬤ PAINLESS

In a big month you've got about two hours of maintenance to do over 30 days. When you entertain at your Memorial Day barbecue, your guests will wonder how you got the house in such great shape in the few months since your New Year's Eve party.

- Spot-clean carpet: 20-30 minutes
- GFI check: five minutes
- Clean refrigerator coils: 10 minutes
- Clean range hood filters: 10 minutes
- Drain hot water tank: 10 minutes

What about materials? The list isn't too exotic:

- Furnace filters
- Lubricating oil
- Spray silicone
- Baking soda and vinegar
- Paint and a foam paint brush
- Carpet cleaner
- Charcoal filter for range hood

February will take even less time, since you're skipping the furnace motor, the refrigerator coils, the garage door, and the water heater, but repeating everything else. The charcoal filters in your range hood will stay put since they only get replaced once or twice a year (read the manufacturer's recommendations). And some tasks, like vacuuming the heat registers, will be part of your normal house cleaning. No extra time needed to get the vacuum cleaner out and set up. Same with checking the GFIs, since you'll be in the bathroom and kitchen at some point anyway. Your house maintenance will be something like the nickname for New Orleans, the Big Easy, but without the Mardi Gras parade.

March will add a few things, depending on how warm and dry it is in your part of the country. You can figure that you'll have to:

1. Clean the gutters.

2. Check the roof for any needed repairs, loose shingles, or damage.

3. Clean your window screens.

4. Inspect your window glazing and caulking.

Cleaning the gutters—if you live anywhere but Death Valley—is essential at least twice a year, especially if you have wood gutters. Standing water can corrode the seams. If enough water accumulates, it can overflow during a rain storm onto your siding and start to lift the paint. Repainting is a lot more work than cleaning the gutters! Take the lazy way out and scoop out winter's debris and hose your gutters down.

Make a note of any cracked or missing window glazing and caulking. You'll have to repair it when the weather warms. Do the same for any missing or damaged roof shingles, too. Unless you have leaks, these repairs can also wait.

Spring Is Just Around the Corner

This may be true except in parts of Montana and the Yukon. You've already cleaned the window screens so they can go up anytime. Your furnace use will be winding down, so you'll be able to skip the filter cleanings soon. April through June will bring more outside

Congratulations! You've managed to write up the first three months' worth of scheduling without getting writer's cramp or going into denial. Being a homeowner isn't so bad after all! When you think of how quickly your work will go, it seems like child's play.

The Lazy Way

maintenance, but that's okay. You'll be all ready for summer barbecues.

Your regular monthly chores will continue. These include:

1. Cleaning your drains.

2. Touching up the interior paint.

3. Checking your GFIs.

4. Cleaning carpet stains.

5. Cleaning your range hood filters.

Your gutters are clean and should stay that way until around Thanksgiving when they fill up with leaves again (if you have a lot of trees around, you may have to clean more often). That's not too bad, only two cleanings a year! Compare that to how much time you spend washing your car!

Check your list of windows and replace any missing glazing. Be sure to paint the glazing after it has cured for at least a week. Painting will protect it and save you the trouble of replacing it next year. In this case, painting is the lazy way out.

Inspect your window trim and other exterior trim for loose or failed caulking. Apply new caulk and paint.

The weather is warming up, flowers are on their way, and that means some yard work. Put the following on your spring list:

1. Rake out the thatch from your lawn.

2. Rake out flower beds.

3. Wash the exterior of the house.

IF YOU'RE SO
INCLINED

If any of your shingles blew off during the winter or were otherwise damaged, they will need to be repaired or replaced. If you're not comfortable doing this, call a reliable roofer and let it go. Have the rest of your roof inspected.

4. Touch up exterior paint.

5. Install screens.

6. Wash and re-seal deck.

7. Begin air conditioning maintenance and yearly professional inspection and servicing.

8. Clean out clothes dryer exhaust vent and any duct work.

It's a good idea to "thatch" your lawn and remove all the dead material—something like brushing out your Old English Sheepdog. Instead of a brush full of fur, you get piles of old grass and bits of leaves and twigs. You can do this with a short-tooth rake and spend hours communing with nature, or you can rent a thatching machine and do it quickly and more thoroughly. Easier yet, hire it out. The same guys who mow lawns often do thatching pretty inexpensively.

It would be great to use the same machine on the flower beds to clean out all the leaves and other seasonal junk, but you would probably be accused of plant abuse by any surviving victims of your botanical carnage. You'll have to resort to hand raking or hired hands. Clean it out, bag the debris, and you're done. While you're at it, you'll be doing air conditioning maintenance, too, when you clear away leaves and clippings from the compressor, an easy two-for-one off of your list!

The dreaded lawn mowing season will also be starting, so be sure your mower is in good shape. Or, take the really easy way out and schedule a lawn service.

QUICK n' PAINLESS

Okay, if you want a little spring color without a ton of work, plant some crocus and tulip bulbs in the fall. They're fun to look at, and disappear after they blossom. Some will die off year to year, but quite a few will survive.

Bath Time

Start out fresh. Soap up the outside of your house and give it a scrub and a rinse. Wash away the winter grime, extend the life of your paint, and clean your windows at the same time—a combo plate special for your home. House washers (please see Chapter 9) are the perfect tool: inexpensive, easy to use, and no rental costs for compressors and pressure washers. Do one side a day or the entire house at once. This is the hassle-free alternative to painting if your existing paint is intact, but just dirty.

When the rains are gone and the sun is going to stick around for awhile, scrub and clean your deck with an appropriate deck cleaner and coat with a sealer (see Chapter 11). Then set out your deck chairs and enjoy the weather.

If you start using your air conditioning, clean the filters monthly.

The Aftermath

Give your house several days to dry. Better yet, give it until the following weekend and check it for any paint problems. Scrape and prime the affected areas and cover with two coats of paint. You can put off painting—a big, time consuming job—for years if you keep the maintenance up.

It's a Trap!

The lint trap in your clothes dryer is evidence that your clothes are slowly disintegrating, but it doesn't catch everything. The exhaust heat from your dryer blows out

via some duct work. Every six months, remove the vent from the outside end of this duct and clean off the lint that tried to escape to the outside for a better life. Place the end of a vacuum cleaner hose down the duct and clean inside as well. If you have really long duct work, you may have to start at the dryer end and blow it out with an electric blower or leaf blower.

Summer in the City

It's time to play, so you want to keep your maintenance to a minimum. Your yard can take as much of your time as you want it to depending on what you plant and whether you hire a lawn service or not. If you can budget for it, have someone else cut the lawn.

At this point, the gutters are still clean, the house has been washed, your screens are up, the interior maintenance goes on, the yard is cleaned up—you're in good shape! You have a few summer things to do:

1. In July, drain off the water heater as you did in January.

2. Continue air conditioning maintenance.

3. Have your heating system serviced before heating season begins.

Having a technician run your heating system through the paces seems weird when it's still 80 degrees outside. But it's easier to do it in September than it is during the first blizzard of the season, when summer's long gone and you're huddling around a space heater because the furnace isn't running. Do it, get it over with, and forget about it.

QUICK **m** *PAINLESS*

Your ever-demanding yard is going to want to be watered. The best time is early morning before it gets too hot, and water evaporates immediately. Late evening can lead to root rot. Let the water run while you get ready for work, and that's it.

All Fall Down

In hot climates, trees are nature's air conditioners. They provide shade and keep our homes cool. They also fill up the yard and gutters with leaves and twigs and other arboreal keepsakes. The last three months of the year will call for picking up the pace a little, but this will be pretty painless. Some fall jobs are:

1. Wash the exterior.

2. Clean the gutters.

3. Have the chimney cleaned and inspected as needed.

4. Inspect the roof.

5. Remove and store the window screens.

6. Clean out the clothes dryer exhaust vent and duct work.

It's tough to make absolute rules about chimney cleanings. It depends on how often you use your chimney and what you're burning. Green, low-grade wood will leave more deposits than seasoned firewood. Talk with a local chimney sweep and describe your situation. If it's an older house you've recently purchased and the former owner can't remember ever seeing a chimney sweep up on the roof, call someone immediately.

It's also time to give the house another bath to wash off all the auto pollution from the summer when everyone was out cruising. Check for any siding damage or missing caulking at the same time and repair as needed. One more trip to the gutters and you'll be done with them until the following spring.

I used to know a software programmer who never did any house maintenance. All he did was write code. When he decided to sell his house, his agent sent a handy guy over to spiff the place up before they put it on the market. Among other things he found a virtual society of pigeons and squirrels living in the attic, gutters with small seedlings growing in them, and a tub drain so clogged it took four hours for the water to empty. The owner had simply stopped taking baths and switched to the basement shower. On his agent's advice he moved to a condominium with a service contract, and has been happily coding away ever since.

It's only easy to skip or ignore your house maintenance for a while, then it's a big headache. There's nothing lazy about clearing ice out of your gutters in freezing weather because the water can't drain through the junk you didn't clean out earlier. It's hands down simpler to spend a little time up front than a lot of miserable time later. These are painless chores and they'll stay that way if they get done on time and done completely. There isn't a heating technician alive who doesn't have stories to tell of expensive repairs that could have been avoided with regular, yearly service and inspections.

Join the ranks of smart home owners. Take care of the small stuff as you go along and spend the rest of your time relaxing and enjoying your well-kept house!

A COMPLETE WASTE OF TIME

The 3 Worst Things to Do When Planning Maintenance

1. Ignore your schedule.

2. Do the work partway.

3. Skip tasks.

Getting Sense on Your Side

The Crazy Way	The Lazy Way
Having the November rains blow in and remembering that the gutters need cleaning: Try to look cute in a yellow rain slicker	Checking your calendar and doing the job in drier weather: How dry I am!
Never cleaning your dryer duct:6 hours to dry 3 T-shirts?	Blow it out twice yearly: Another full load dry in record time
Repainting your dirty house: Man, I had to wash it before I painted anyway!	Regular washing: I wash, I am, now I can scram
Ignoring the roof until it leaks during a rain storm: Yikes! The sound of dripping water drives me crazy!	Doing roof inspections in warm, dry weather: Ah, the tranquil sound of water rolling into the gutters
Buying materials you think you'll need to care of your house: What's wrong with having a few extra bags of concrete around?	Go to the store, take list for specific tasks in hand:All done in no time flat
Never making, or following, a maintenance schedule: Hey, was I supposed to get married today?	Life has never been better since I wrote up and followed my Lazy maintenance schedule

More Lazy Stuff

A

How to Get Someone Else to Do It

WHEN THE GOING GETS TOUGH, GET A CONTRACTOR

Life is short. Even if you believe in repeated reincarnations, you might as well enjoy them, not spend them all repainting your cedar siding and replacing your roof. A competent contractor may be your answer.

There are ardent do-it-yourselfers who never hire anything out. They usually truly enjoy doing the work and/or saving the money. If you're not one of them, and would rather spend your money than your time on your house, then you need to hire some of the big jobs out. Some big jobs include:

1. House painting

2. Floor refinishing

3. Building a deck

4. Roofing

5. Gutter repairs

1. Anyone can paint, but how badly do you want to haul yourself up two or three stories and brush on gallon after gallon of colonial white? A painting crew will bring ladders, planks, and probably spray equipment. They can cover more in one day than you will in a week of squeezing in a few hours after work.

2. Floor refinishing is wretched work. The fumes can be overwhelming, and fine, powdery dust goes everywhere. You can't learn how to handle a floor sander effectively on the first try and may well end up doing more gouging than sanding. This is a hard job, and well worth hiring out.

3. There's more to building a deck than meets the eye, especially if it's a second-story job. There are structural requirements and code requirements for railings you must meet for safe results. The builder needs an assortment of power tools, levels, chalk lines, and myriad hand tools. Is this what you want to spend your weekends working on, or do you want to lounge around on a finished deck?

4. Roofing? Forget it! Roofers are very hard workers, more so than floor finishers. If the old roof has to be stripped off, you definitely want a roofing contractor to do the work.

5. Install-them-yourself plastic gutters are a mediocre second choice to continuous aluminum gutters. Slope them improperly, and watch the fun when they back up and overflow. A competent gutter contractor can work wonders.

Making Contact

As a homeowner, you have to decide what's in your best interest. You can do any of the jobs listed above and learn to do them well. Or you can work extra hours at your regular job, one that you do well and like, and use the extra cash to pay another professional to work on your house. Which is the best choice for you?

The laziest thing to do might be to take out a short-term loan and pay it off later. Some choice—fill out a loan application or dangle from ladders with a paint brush. If you decide to hire a contractor (applause), how do you go about finding one?

You have a number of avenues open to you. The best people are found by word of mouth. You can ask:

1. Co-workers

2. Your real estate agent

3. Your banker

4. Neighbors

Ask several friends and acquaintances questions about contractors they've hired, such as:

1. What work did the contractor do?

2. Was the job on time and within budget?

3. Would you hire this contractor again?

After you've narrowed your list, set up appointments to discuss the scope of the job and get bids. If you're absolutely new to this, ask the contractor a lot of questions, such as:

1. Are you licensed and bonded?

2. Are there any liens against you?

3. What kind of products will you use and why?

4. Will you stay on the job until completion?

5. Who will be in charge, you or an employee?

6. What kind of warranty do you offer?

7. Will we have a contract?

9. How will I make the payment?

If every contractor tells you something different, you may want to consult an architect, but, even then, you may hear different opinions. Generally, though, unless your project presents some bizarre challenges, bidding should be pretty straightforward.

State laws require contractors to be licensed and bonded. A bond is a guaranteed amount of cash a contractor or bonding company can be asked to forfeit to a client who wins a legal case over incompetent or uncompleted work. It gives the customer some protection and leverage. A lien is a claim against the bond.

It may be easier to hire an unlicensed contractor, but, later on, it could be harder to get the job finished properly—if at all! If an unlicensed individual is injured while working on your house, you effectively can be considered the employer of the injured party and, therefore, the target of legal action. Do you want to wind up in court when all you were trying to do was get your roof fixed?

The products contractors use vary depending on the job, the budget, and the preferences of both the contractor and the customer. Oil paint or latex? Fiberglass shingles or asphalt? Plywood or particle board? Get some justification for the product choices your contractor makes to be sure you agree. And don't be talked into the wrong choice, even if it's less expensive. An inferior product could fail prematurely, and you could find yourself going through the whole process all over again!

It's your house, so you'd really like it if your contractor would drop everything else and run right over. This is not realistic, but a schedule you can both agree to is. You should set one up and then stick to it. There will always be some allowances made for unforeseen problems and weather considerations, but a final, no excuses finish date should be established at the outset.

Many contractors start off working alone, or with a very small crew, and build their reputations based on their personal participation in the work. As their businesses grow, many of them become managers and estimators, and end up doing little or no work in the field, that is, on the house itself. Be clear about who will be in charge of your job and what you expect. Know who will be doing the actual labor and that it is in agreement with what the contractor who was recommended to you guaranteed.

Warranties vary. Labor and installation may have one warranty, the product itself another. It can get murky if, for instance, paint fails after two months. Who's to blame? The painters? The product? The painter is ultimately responsible, but may try to bring the manufacturer into the fray. This isn't your problem, of course, but it may complicate the issue and delay completion of the job.

Some contractors are very casual about contracts, and others use a multi-page boiler plate to cover just about everything short of an errant jet airliner dropping its engine onto your roof. Do you need a contract? At a minimum, write up a letter of agreement. It should include:

1. Scope of the work

2. Work schedule

3. Payment schedule

4. Warranty

Don't worry about insulting by asking for a written agreement. Spelling out the terms in writing is in everyone's best interest. For most straightforward jobs, such as painting your living room, it's not all that necessary, but it can't hurt anything. Protect your interests and keep it in writing.

Agree to a payment schedule in advance. Unless you have a disagreement about the value of the work completed, you should stick to it and pay up promptly. Cash flow is critical to self-employed contractors and even a few days' delay can hurt.

Unless you're doing an extensive remodel, you'll have easy experiences on single jobs with competent contractors. They'll do their job, clean up, and leave. And you'll get to enjoy the results without the labor and anxiety. That's easy living!

If You Want to Learn More, Read These

Books

Bennett, Allegra. *Renovating Woman: A Guide to Home Repair, Maintenance, and Real Men.* Pocket Books, 1997.

Broecker, William L. (editor), James A. Hufnagel, and Dean Johnson. *The Stanley Complete Step-By-Step Book of Home Repair and Improvement.* Simon & Schuster, 1993.

Decosse, Cy. *Black & Decker Home Improvement Library: How Things Get Done.* Cowles Creative Publishing, 1996.

The Family Handyman Helpful Hints: Quick and Easy Solutions/Time Saving Tips/Tricks of the Trade. Readers Digest, 1995.

52 Easy Weekend Home Repairs: A Year's Worth of Money Saving Projects. Time-Life Books, 1998.

1001 Do-It-Yourself Hints & Tips: Tricks, Shortcuts, How-Tos & Other Nifty Ideas for Inside, Outside, & All Around the House. Readers Digest, 1998.

Web sites

http://www.homespot.com (writer John Maines of the Florida Sun-Sentinel answers your home repair and related questions)

http://www.toiletology.com (a site devoted to—what else?—toilets and toilet repairs)

http://homearts.com (*Good Housekeeping's* site)

http://www.bhglive.com (*Better Homes and Gardens*)

http://www.soundhome.com (certified home inspector George Guttman's construction, remodeling, and home maintenance site)

http://www.todayshomeowner.com

http://www.hometime.com

http://YourNewHouse.com

http://www.doityourself.com

Some Web sites come and go and there are no guarantees how long these will survive in the cyberjungle. You can always do a search under "home repair" or "do it yourself," as well as specific topics like "plumbing" or "roof."

Magazines

Old House Journal
Sunset
This Old House

If You Don't Know What It Means/Does, Look Here

Amps: Short for Ampere, fun French physicist (1775-1836); a unit of electric current; only pertinence to you and your home is that your fuses and circuit breakers are rated in amps.

Belt sander: Electric sander that uses a continuous belt of sand paper.

Casement window: Swings out like a door.

Caulking: Sealant and filler, comes in tubes; various types, all potentially messy and sticky to deal with.

Circuit: A path of electricity, from beginning to end.

Circular saw: Electric saw with a circular, rotating blade; excellent for rough cutting (and for personal injuries if used carelessly).

Deck screws: Coated exterior screws used for securing decking in lieu of nails.

Disc sander: Electric sander with rotating disc.

Double hung window: The type that slides up and down; usually painted shut in old houses.

Downspout: A vertical section of pipe that attaches to a gutter to drain water away from a house.

Drain trap: U-shaped drain pipe with a tendency to clog unless flushed regularly; constructed to trap water so sewer gases stay out of your home.

Drywall: Wallboard or plasterboard; prefabricated sheets of plaster-type material for building walls.

French drain: Pit or trench filled with some kind of crushed stone.

Galvanized: Coated with zinc to resist rusting.

Glazing compound: Putty-like material for sealing glass to a sash; maintains a seal against wind and water on old windows.

Ground fault circuit interrupter, or GFI: Funny looking outlet in bathrooms, kitchens, and often outside designed to detect minor leaks or irregularities in electrical current and then shut off immediately.

Grounded: A good idea for your electrical system; protects you from shocks.

Grout: Mortar used to seal tile joints and other masonry.

Joists: Horizontal boards, 2" x 6" or larger, that support floors and ceilings.

Landscapers: The only people who should ever mow your lawn.

Latex paint: Uses water as its base and solvent; most common paint used in residential work.

Lath: Strips of wood over which plaster is applied.

Lead-based paint: Considered the epitome of old-house evils; lead was outlawed as a common paint ingredient in the late 1970s; use caution when working around it.

Mortar: A mixture of cement, lime, sand, and other fun stuff, used to set bricks and other masonry.

Plunger: Something you ought to have in your bathrooms to unclog toilets and stopped-up sinks.

Polarized receptacle: Modern receptacle designed to accommodate plugs with two different sized prongs for grounding purposes.

Rafters: Angled framing that supports a roof.

Receptacle: The thing in the wall that you plug stuff into.

Sash control: A piece of spring metal that replaces missing or broken ropes in double-hung windows.

Service panel: Electrical panel containing circuit breakers or fuses.

Shakes/shingles: Roofing materials, also used as siding materials in some cases.

Short circuit: One activity that blows a fuse or trips a breaker.

Spackle: Thin plaster-like material used for patching holes in walls; also, a word unknown to computer spell checkers.

Stucco: An exterior plaster-type finish applied over lath; a slang way of indicating you're sticking to something.

Studs: Vertical wood framing in a wall; the boards to which plaster and wallboard are attached.

Swedish finish: Tough, film-forming wood floor finish; also a schizophrenic Scandinavian.

Valley: On roofs, where two slopes meet.

Water shutoff: Turns off all the water in the house; a good thing to know about before a pipe bursts in the dead of winter.

D

It's Time for Your Reward

Taking care of our homes is like a grown up version of cleaning our rooms as kids, or attempting to, except that there aren't any parental enforcers around. The only master of ceremonies we can get to give out the prizes is the one staring back at us in the bathroom mirror, right above the drain we just unclogged. But that's not so bad. At least we can choose the reward. No restrictions on how big an ice cream sundae to order this time and, yes, I'll take a double shot of whipped cream, please!

Reward Table

Task	Reward
Clean the gutters	Espresso and a pastry
Wash the siding	Rent trashy videos
Seal the deck	Go to the zoo and look at the seals
Polish the wood floors	Schedule a massage
Repair window putty	Take a long nap . . . with a friend
Complete monthly maintenance	Dance the night away

Task	Reward
Clean the yard	Mix up a pitcher of margaritas
Touch up the walls	Go to a ball game
Flush your drains	Make a cheesecake
Patch vinyl floor	Go hot tubbing
Buy house tools	Buy something for you!

Where to Find What You're Looking For

Now you can do these tasks, too!
The Lazy Way ™

Starting to think there are a few more of life's little tasks that you've been putting off? Don't worry—we've got you covered. Take a look at all of *The Lazy Way* books available. Just imagine—you can do almost anything *The Lazy Way!*

Clean Your House The Lazy Way
By Barbara H. Durham
0-02-862649-4

Cook Your Meals The Lazy Way
By Sharon Bowers
0-02-862644-3

Handle Your Money The Lazy Way
By Sarah Young Fisher and Carol Turkington
0-02-862632-X

Train Your Dog The Lazy Way
By Andrea Arden
0-87605180-8

Take Care of Your Car The Lazy Way
By Michael Kennedy and Carol Turkington
0-02-862647-8

Learn Spanish The Lazy Way
By Vivian Isaak and Bogumila Michalewicz
0-02-862650-8

*All Lazy Way books are just $12.95!

additional titles on the back!

Build Your Financial Future The Lazy Way

By Terry Meany

0-02-862648-6

Shed Some Pounds The Lazy Way

By Annette Cain and Becky Cortopassi-Carlson

0-02-862999-X

Organize Your Stuff The Lazy Way

By Toni Ahlgren

0-02-863000-9

Feed Your Kids Right The Lazy Way

By Virginia Van Vynckt

0-02-863001-7

Cut Your Spending The Lazy Way

By Leslie Haggin

0-02-863002-5

Stop Aging The Lazy Way

By Judy Myers, Ph.D.

0-02-862793-8

Get in Shape The Lazy Way

By Annette Cain

0-02-863010-6

Learn French The Lazy Way

By Christophe Desmaison

0-02-863011-4

Learn Italian The Lazy Way

By Gabrielle Euvino

0-02-863014-9

Keep Your Kids Busy The Lazy Way

By Barbara Nielsen and Patrick Wallace

0-02-863013-0